OVER MY DEAD BODIES

from the lab to the slab

~

Dr Andrew Adam FRCPath

Over My Dead Bodies

Copyright © 2024 by Andrew Adam

All rights reserved.
No part of this publication may be
reproduced or transmitted in any form, or by any means,
electronic or mechanical, including photocopying, recording
or by any information storage and retrieval system, without
prior written permission from the author.

Edited by Kate Harris
Illustrations by Dr Jeanette Cayley
Cover image by Freepik

*To my wife, Jacqui, who has always believed in me.
She has been my encourager, keel and stabilizer
in every situation.*

*Much to her relief, I would definitely
not conduct her autopsy.*

The Author

Andrew Adam is a retired pathologist who has pursued an unconventional and zigzag career as a Times' journalist, male model, Middlesex medical student, RAF medical officer, NHS consultant, pastor, police chaplain, freelance writer, and guest speaker on Cunard cruise ships. He and his wife Jacqui live in Taunton, Somerset, and have recently celebrated their 60th wedding anniversary.

Other books by the author include:
Beechwoods and Bayonets (1983). Barracuda Books.
Thomas Cochrane and the Dragon Throne (2018). SPCK.

Contents

Acknowledgements		vii
Introduction		ix
1	Where have all the Flowers Gone?	1
2	Family Roots	5
3	Death of a Small Civilization	10
4	Epsom, Oxford and Fleet Street	15
5	Medical Starting Line	24
6	Carrying on Regardless	31
7	Clerks and Dressers	41
8	Taking the Queen's Shilling	50
9	Licensed to Kill	62
10	Salisbury General Infirmary	75
11	Near-Death Experiences	83
12	Rites of Passage	92
13	Station Medical Officer	100
14	Pathology Training	111
15	Fen Dwellers	120
16	Setting a New Course	135
17	Ay Eff Eye Pee	144
18	Going in for Trade	155
19	Musgrove Park Hospital	163
20	Down Among the Dead Men	176
21	Coping (and not Coping)	189
22	Murder at Sea	194
Afterword		202

Acknowledgements

Many people have touched and influenced my life, nearly all of them for the better, and the principal ones are in this book. In a few cases I have changed or withheld their names. I hope my gratitude to them (including the ones who are now dead) shows through.

Let me single out those who encouraged me to write my story. Foremost is Jacqui, who has been the centre of my life for more than sixty years; we celebrated our diamond wedding anniversary in December 2023. She is a pillar of love and support and without her I would never have qualified in medicine. She sacrificed her own plans for a career in order to raise our family. My own career was sinuous if not zigzag, and she adapted without complaint to every change of direction, including seventeen house moves.

Then there are our three children, Rob, Kate and Lizby. When they were growing up, my work was a mystery to them because I spoke little about it. I had no idea how peeved that left them until recently, when they badgered me for an account. Kate's practical assistance has been invaluable; she is an accomplished author and critic, plus she has inside knowledge. Without her help I might have fallen at the first fence. I am also greatly indebted to the professional skills of Alison Hull and Donna Hillyer.

My children's recollections of family events are fresher than mine; they have corrected some errors and provided a sense of balance. They have also shown me how often I took my family for granted and I hope I am forgiven for that.

My final thanks go to Dr Jeanette Cayley who drew the illustrations; she is the secretary of the Medical Art Society and a friend from way back. When I edited our hospital journal sixty years ago, she brightened its pages with her line drawings. They are as charming and humorous now as they were then.

Introduction

Most non-medical people have a distorted view of pathology. They believe it is exclusively about dead bodies and that pathologists are high priests of death, cool and detached to the point of freakishness. Since my earliest days of training, friends often asked me, 'Why on earth did you choose *that* for a living?'

Television drama and films are largely responsible. Their pathologists are involved almost entirely in violent deaths, and they are highly professional: super-efficient, cynical, and lacking in compassion. But, leaving aside the inaccuracy of that portrayal, they form a tiny part of the whole. The UK has more than 11,000 pathologists and only a handful are forensic specialists.

The truth is that pathology is a vast and expanding empire which embraces many sub-specialties. The Royal College of Pathologists describes it in universal terms as 'the science behind the cure.' It extends from the historic big four (haematology, chemical pathology, microbiology and histopathology) to transfusion science, toxicology, immunogenetics and molecular pathology. Some of the new arrivals are so esoteric that their practitioners barely understand each other's language.

Thus there is no such thing as a typical pathologist, but the figure who best corrects the popular misconception is the histopathologist. I practised in that specialty for many years in the Royal Air Force and the National Health Service. Histopathology is the study and diagnosis of diseases at a cellular level using a light microscope and it is vital to cancer treatment. It is traditionally wed to morbid anatomy, the study of diseases in dead bodies. It is a marriage of logic as well as convenience.

Histopathologists are therefore hospital doctors who alternate between the lab and the slab. When they are not engaged in more congenial work, they face horrific scenes in the mortuary and do things that no other hospital doctor is expected to do.

What sort of people are they? They are human beings like other doctors, with the same senses and weaknesses. They have an exacting and well-paid job which is often unsavoury but never dull. They are pragmatic; they will recount their most famous or infamous cases with gory details and no abstract speculation. Their sleep is untroubled by existential questions. They spend a lot of time in the company of dead people, but in my experience most of them understand no more about life and death than the next man.

I have written this book as a counterbalance. Not all pathologists are the same, and some like me have a different approach to the work. None of my cases were famous and I do not enjoy gore. On the other hand, existential questions and the human predicament fascinate me. In the mortuary I struggled constantly with the cruelty and capriciousness of death, and the mystery of what one medical author has described as 'life after life.'

In my middle age I became ill and burned out. I nearly quit pathology, but something remarkable happened. I found a faith which turned my worldview upside down. It enabled me to continue in the work and it helped me to understand something about pain and suffering. Nonetheless I struggle with them still, like everyone who has ever drawn breath.

A final misconception is that pathologists are just scientists. In fact, they must all have a medical degree and undergo years of clinical training before becoming laboratory-based. That gives them a worm's eye view of medicine.

And, believe me, they know their worms.

1

Where have all the Flowers Gone?

On a summer's day, fifty years ago, Heathrow teemed like an ant hill that had been given a good poking. The airport roads bustled with cars and vans and thousands of travellers scurried in and out of its buildings. Every sixty seconds a plane headed down a runway and the hum became a roar.

As you approached it on the old A25, everything seemed to be in good order, as if nothing ominous could happen there. Yet two days earlier a Trident airliner belonging to British European Airways had dropped out of the sky less than three minutes after taking off. There were 118 people on board, and none survived the crash.

Today this colossal tragedy is known as the Staines Air Disaster. It took place on the 18th of June 1972 and remains the most lethal accident in UK aviation history after the Lockerbie bombing in 1988.

The day after it happened, a senior RAF colleague and I arrived at Heathrow and made our way to Building No. 461. It was a bonded warehouse that had been set apart for a special purpose.

'Your IDs please, gentlemen!' We were in military uniform, but reporters were everywhere, and the security people were taking no chances. We presented our identity cards and were checked against a list. Stooping under the police tape, we passed from the sunshine into a vast cavern lit by arc lamps.

It was a house of horrors. In the centre were four trestle tables covered in black plastic sheets. Plastic-clad figures were working at them. Buckets and hosepipes stood alongside. The floor was covered in inches of blood-soaked sawdust. Along a wall, scores of coffins waited to be filled.

A truck fitted with a cage was parked inside the warehouse. It held battered suitcases, handbags, clothes, shoes and personal effects. The acrid smell of burnt plastic mingled with the smell of death.

My mouth was dry and the hairs on my neck stood on end; this situation was entirely new to me. I'd never conducted a post-mortem examination, and the ones that I had attended as a medical student were teaching sessions, on patients who died of natural causes. They took place in a controlled environment. The pathologists paraded their knowledge with bravura and quizzed the students continuously; we responded by showing our ignorance. It was quite convivial and light-hearted.

Now I was a medical officer in the RAF with orders to attend this ghastly event as an observer. The cause of the disaster was unknown; for all that we knew, the passengers could have been the victims of a mass murder.

Home Office and RAF pathologists were assisting the Air Investigation Branch (AIB) in its task, and they worked in almost complete silence. They used a production line approach which had been tried and tested over many years. One by one, bodies and parts of bodies were conveyed in refrigerated trucks from the crash site to the building. They were measured, photographed and x-rayed before being dissected. The work was divided between the four tables.

A separate group of investigators worked in an office inside the warehouse, intent on one thing: identifying the victims. They were AIB staff, undertakers, dental experts, police officers and airport officials. Their job was to correlate the pathologists' findings with the other evidence. The undertakers came from J.H. Kenyon, a well-known London firm which had years of experience of mass disasters of every kind, from earthquakes to night club fires.

A bank of phones rang frequently as the investigators consulted a set of wall charts. The passengers' names were written along the horizontal axis and the identifying factors along the vertical axis. Each chart resembled a giant game of noughts and crosses.

Surrounded by the mess and horror, each investigator worked with cool unhurried efficiency. As I watched, a man in shirtsleeves hung up a phone and wrote something on a clipboard. He called to a supervisor, 'Over here sir, please!' They studied his findings and consulted a sheaf of papers. Checking, constantly checking.

Finally, the supervisor nodded and the man filled in a space on the chart. The right number of critical questions had been answered; a body could be signed off and another coffin could be filled. There were no congratulations or acknowledgement, just a flicker of relief on tired faces.

Today, identifying bodies is far easier because DNA matching provides an absolute test (though it may present difficulties in application). In 1972 there was no DNA matching. Pathologists used fingerprints, palm prints, dental charts and hospital records, as well as prostheses and cardiac pacemakers which carry unique reference numbers.

They also used secondary markers like jewellery, passports and distinctive clothing. At Heathrow every piece of cloth or leather and every laundry tag was labelled and placed in a plastic bag. Scars, tattoos, old fractures and surgical operations were carefully recorded and photographed.

I had never imagined a disaster on this scale and the sight of the fragmented, burned and commingled bodies was sickening. But the atmosphere was so intense and purposeful that I put my feelings on hold and joined vicariously in the investigation. All that the pathologists were doing was identifying bodies, but as a human being I sensed how vital that work was to devastated relatives and how awful it must be to have no remains to grieve over and to bury.

The more complex question of what caused the crash would take months to resolve and the post-mortem findings on the senior pilot would be of critical importance. That part of the story comes later in this book.

The examinations took several days to complete. That evening my wing commander colleague and I emerged from the building. The heat had gone out of the day and the ant hill had quietened down. We walked across the tarmac to his car. Reaction had set in; he was feeling relaxed, and I was in turmoil.

'Remarkably smooth operation, don't you think?' he said, feeling for his keys.

I was miles away. A hearse had drawn up and men were loading a coffin.

'What did you think of the operation?' he repeated. It was a professional question, one doctor comparing notes with another.

'Extraordinary!' I muttered, 'Where on earth did they go?'

'Sorry …?'

'I keep thinking of them with their boarding passes, finding their seats, settling down, then falling … praying, screaming. Where are they now?'

My question hung in the air. Pete Seeger's poignant anti-war song about flowers and the loss of young men drummed in my head. The wing commander (a seasoned pathologist) looked astonished, as if I had admitted to a fondness for necrophilia. We drove home in silence and the matter was not mentioned again.

2

Family Roots

My father's family were crofters and agricultural labourers in Denny near Stirling in Scotland. Few of them moved far away and according to an old guidebook the local graveyards held so many Adam headstones that it was known as the Garden of Eden.

My grandfather John Adam broke the mould. He was born in 1869 and left school at twelve. At sixteen he had a menial job in a paper mill which he hated. One day he swore that he would become a doctor or 'die in the attempt.' It was a turning point; without it I might have grown up herding bullocks and this book would not have been written.

I remember him as a small terrier-like man with twinkling eyes, a bushy moustache, and an accent as thick as a bannock cake. He typified the many Scots who have escaped poverty through hard work and self-improvement. Despite great difficulties, he won a place at Glasgow Medical School at nineteen and qualified as a doctor in 1892.

He married a local girl called Agnes Paterson; she had Danish blood and intense pale blue eyes which their children inherited. The couple moved to Yorkshire, where John practised as a GP. There the so-called 'Adam curse' descended and blighted their happiness. To explain the reason, I must digress.

At the beginning of the 20th century, tuberculosis was the greatest single killer in Britain. There was no effective treatment and no protection until vaccinations started in the 1940s. I had no idea of the devastating impact of the disease on my family until my daughter, Kate, unearthed an intriguing document on the internet a few years ago. It was the MD thesis which John Adam submitted to Glasgow University in

1914, titled *The Treatment of Advanced Phthisis*. Phthisis, like consumption, is an old word for tuberculosis.

In the paper he described a number of his patients and they included several of his relatives. I was shocked to learn that four and possibly five of his six siblings died of TB. Two were younger brothers who came to his home in Yorkshire in the terminal stages of the disease and died there under his care.

Of the younger lad, who was 21 years old, he wrote: 'The patient was treated in the same house and under the same conditions as his older brother. During suitable weather he was wheeled out to a grass-covered plot in the adjoining orchard. Here he lay resting under the shade of the blossoming fruit trees, whose healthy condition proclaimed the purity of the atmosphere. But in spite of his ardent wish to live ... his constitution utterly failed to make even temporary progress towards improvement.'

The deaths of so many loved ones in their prime must have affected John and Agnes deeply. You can sense the current of grief running through his thesis. And they probably feared for their own children. The Yorkshire coalfields where John practised were rife with lung diseases. Shortly before the outbreak of the First World War he moved his family to London and eventually set up in practice in Kensington.

He died in 1947 and neither *The Lancet* nor the *British Medical Journal* carried an obituary notice, so I know little about his professional life. I inherited a silver inkwell inscribed by a grateful patient and his gold half-hunter watch, but they hold no clues. John did, however, have a clever ruse for expectant mothers which my father loved to describe. After making his examination, he would predict the sex of the baby according to what he thought would please the mother more. But when he booked her confinement, he wrote down the *other* sex against the delivery date. So, if his verbal prediction proved wrong, he could appeal to the diary and be proved right.

Infallibility, however acquired, is an admirable quality in a physician. It never fails to inspire confidence.

My grandfather was a highflyer. He pursued postgraduate degrees like a bounty hunter, and he put his two sons, a daughter and an older brother through medicine. He chivvied them all continuously about their studies and when my father Robert (who was known as Bob) sat for an Oxford scholarship in 1923 he wisely kept quiet about it. Over breakfast he simply announced that he had won the award. His father was speechless with delight. 'All he could do was to give me a hearty blow on the chest.'

Bob went up to University College in Oxford the following year, and there he met my mother, Grace Margaret Ervine. Her father was an Irish manufacturer called William Ervine, a self-made man whose lack of education concealed shrewd business acumen. He married late and was desperate for a son to inherit his leather factory, but my grandmother produced only girls.

My mother was the fifth of six daughters and by the time she arrived Grandfather William was fed up with the whole business of procreation. The need to find six husbands and dowries did not improve his temper, which was naturally dour and judgmental.

A spiritual pall hung over the household like the odour of animal urine over the tanning vats in William's leather factory. He belonged to the exclusive Plymouth Brethren and his first concern was to deny his daughters everything pleasurable. That included worldly music, worldly books and magazines, the cinema, cosmetics and card games. The girls were not even permitted to sew on Sundays. Drinking alcohol and smoking were Satan's sport.

In later life my mother wrote articles for the BBC and ladies' journals. In one of them she described the agony the girls suffered during Brethren meetings. There was no programme or liturgy, just a harmonium to accompany the singing. A man would 'speak if the Spirit moved him' and if the Spirit was silent everyone stared silently at the floor. The meetings dragged on so long that Mother came to understand the meaning of the word eternity, or so she claimed. Other words continued to puzzle her: words like grace, holiness and circumcision.

'Circumcision puzzled me more than all the rest. This word cropped up Sunday after Sunday in St. Paul's letters. Having no brothers, I knew nothing whatever about the matter and all inquiries at home were met with generalisations which left me more baffled. Years later I came to the conclusion it must have something to do with geometry, a subject in which I was very weak.'

She was baptised at the age of fourteen. No fiery tongues descended, and she was left disappointed. The next day she experienced a blaze of another kind, a row with one of her sisters. It shattered any sense of sanctification she may have had.

Soon afterwards something far worse happened. A close family friend and a pillar of the church molested the eldest Ervine daughter sexually. She confided in my mother and the two girls went in fear and trembling to their parents. Such things were inadmissible in polite society. Grandfather William refused to believe the story and punished them for telling wicked lies. The matter was never mentioned again, and the abuser remained a family friend.

The episode left my mother very bitter. 'By the time I was eighteen,' she wrote, 'my belief in God, such as it was, was shattered.' It took years to rebuild.

These brief descriptions show that my parents came from very different backgrounds. Mother was brought up in a home where religion was all important, but it was oppressive and pharisaic. She despised her father and loved her mother. She had an idealized vision of marriage as a fusion of souls, not just of the flesh. It was something for which she yearned all her life but never achieved. She knew little of science or medicine; she was a writer and a romantic.

My father came from a home where religion had little place and medicine was everything. I never recall him speaking of a personal faith, though he never lacked an opinion on the hypocrisy of Christians, particularly his in-laws. He was an intellectual with an analytical brain and an encyclopaedic memory, but few romantic ideas. He was also a fine draughtsman and won prizes for his anatomical drawings. He would have done well in a university science department.

Against all expectation my mother was allowed to try for university, and she won a place at St. Hugh's College, Oxford, to read English Literature. She was the only one of the six girls to get to university. In the carefree atmosphere of Oxford in the flapper era she met my father and they fell in love, though I often wonder whether Mother was simply escaping her nightmarish home.

She rebelled eventually. At Oxford she regularly went to the theatre as part of her studies, and she knew every contemporary play in the English language. Yet Grandfather William forbade his daughters the theatre. One evening while she was living at home, she slid off to see *Journey's End*, the moving play by R.C. Sherriff about the Great War. On return she was confronted in the hall by her angry parent. A furious row ensued, and she stormed out for good.

The young couple kept their engagement secret until after my mother had graduated, and even then, they could not marry until my father qualified. The engagement dragged on into a third and fourth year. It baffles me still that two intelligent people could be engaged for so long and not realise how poorly suited they were.

3

Death of a Small Civilization

Their marriage, which took place in early 1932, immediately came under pressure. They had no home and no money, and my father had to live in hospital quarters to complete his training. When they were finally united, he was a GP assistant in Shepherd's Bush, and they lived with his elder brother and his wife. Both men were doctors and my mother, who was soon pregnant, should have been well looked after. But the brother and sister-in-law were alcoholics and my father worked impossibly long hours.

Years later my mother described her situation as 'pregnant, penniless, in a filthy house with quarrelsome people, ill and neglected by my husband.'

Her baby Julia was born prematurely in May 1934 and lived only eighteen hours. She was buried in an unmarked grave and after Mother's death I found a bill for 7s 6d for the casket among her papers. It was all she had with which to remember her baby. Rightly or wrongly, she harboured a deep resentment at my father for not preventing the death.

They moved to North London where he bought into a partnership with borrowed money. Here my sister Ruth was born in 1936. Father had a list of 2,500 patients and worked effectively on his own. He employed a part-time nurse, a dispenser and a maid who answered the door. But nobody was paid to open the mail, do the accounts, type letters or answer the telephone. All that was my mother's responsibility.

She took great pains in her role, but she felt the injustice of it. Years later she wrote an article titled *The Doctor's Wife's Dilemma* for a ladies' magazine. In it she pointed out that prior to the NHS a GP's wife acted as secretary, nurse, receptionist, chaperone, chauffeur and general factotum. She had no life outside the home and no income of her own, which left her entirely dependent on her husband. At the same time she was raising a family, running a household and trying to keep everyone happy.

When the NHS was introduced in 1948, the male GPs who joined it brought with them approximately 15,000 wives; they were an unpaid labour force equal to a sixth of all hospital staff. Yet in no time they were replaced by professionals, unrecognized and unrewarded. Mother called them the unsung heroines of the old system.

The doctor's house was not simply a place to go for medical treatment; it was a sanctuary and confessional box. During the years of economic depression, a GP dealt not only with sickness but with the consequences of unemployment, poverty and despair. For many patients the workhouse was one pay packet away. If illness struck, they could not afford an ambulance let alone hospital fees. They turned to 'Dr Bob' and threw themselves onto his charity. My mother was philosophical. She wrote: 'The ethos was service not financial gain, and you couldn't blame the patients. Only a fool deliberately refused to pay a doctor's bill. You never knew when you would need his services again.'

I was born in June 1939, three months before Hitler invaded Poland. The war that followed ruined my family. The better-off patients left London, many of them with bills unpaid, and the schools emptied. By the time the so-called Phoney War ended in April 1940, half of the practice had vanished, leaving my father deeply in debt.

He continued working until the army called him up. For more than three years he served as an anaesthetist in Malta, Egypt and Palestine. Much of the time my mother did not know where he was, nor if he were dead or alive.

No one who has not lived through the prolonged bombing of a city can imagine what it is like, especially for a child. We lived in constant fear, especially at night. There were air raids, flying bombs, incendiaries and a constant threat of invasion. All around us were ruined buildings and ruined lives. My sister Ruth and I were evacuated twice to the country, and when our mother's health broke down we were handed like parcels around family and friends. Our schools changed constantly, and life seemed to hang by a thread.

Then in May 1945 there was peace in Europe. Two months later a man in khaki uniform rang the bell of our semi-detached home in North London. A tropical sun had turned his skin to mahogany and bleached his hair. I gaped as he took my mother in his arms and kissed her.

She blushed. 'Andy, this is your father. Come and give him a hug.'

Not on your life! I was barely six years old and I ran off in panic. My sister Ruth, who was three years older, embraced him but to me he was an intruder. All my life my mother had been the centre of my universe: my protector, provider and carer. I wasn't sharing her with anybody, certainly not a stranger with a swagger stick and a Sam Brown belt.

Over the weeks I warmed to Dad as he resumed the headship of the family. I followed him everywhere, even into the bathroom, and he showed me how to wash my hands in a basin like a surgeon, instead of waving them under a cold tap: 'Like this, little man, like this.'

He stropped his cut-throat razor on a strap behind the bathroom door and I marvelled at the sound of stubble being scraped away.

'Will my face be hairy like yours, Daddy?'

'One day it will. And one day you may have my razors if you want them.'

I was mystified by strange noises that came from my mother's bedroom late at night, but when I went to investigate, the door was closed against me.

As soon as he was demobbed, Dad obtained a place in a general practice in Torquay in South Devon. When I realised how far it was from London and that I must say goodbye to my aunts, uncles and cousins and my friends, I was dismayed. But when I learned it was a seaside town with beaches and palm trees, I quite liked the idea.

* * *

Leaving London seemed no great loss. The people were exhausted and malnourished, and the city faced bankruptcy and the huge challenge of rebuilding. We were leaving those troubles behind. At last we would be together as a family, and I would have a new school and new friends. A grand new life beckoned, or so it seemed.

I remember particularly Christmas 1946. In spite of the rationing, Mother managed to get hold of a turkey and all the trimmings for a feast. There was no shortage of hungry mouths to share it. The government was taking its time repatriating thousands of German and Italian prisoners of war. Dad conducted clinics at a nearby POW camp and he invited two young German prisoners to join us.

They looked like scarecrows in their grey fatigues, bowing nervously to my parents. We had no German and they had little English, but over the meal the ice thawed. Afterwards Mother sat at the piano and they sang in fine baritones: *Silent Nacht, Heilige Nacht.*

We joined in the reprise in English until Mother suddenly started sobbing. For five years our nations had inflicted terrible wounds on each other. Now, as the Christmas bells rang out, we were friends once more. 'Peace on earth and good will to all men!'

It is one of my few happy childhood memories, but it was short lived. After the war, an unprecedented number of marriages broke down at all levels of society. My parents had been changed forever by their wartime experiences. The fault lines that were always present in their marriage gaped open. The differences in their world views and spirituality were too great. They were divorced in 1948.

Somebody once described a family break-up as the death of a small civilization. That is how it felt to me at the age of eight. In my innocence I believed that I had been given my family back; now it was stolen away. Who had taken it and why? All I knew was that the people who loved me most in the world, and whom I loved the most, suddenly seemed to hate each other. Was it my fault? Who would look after my sister and me? The sense of powerlessness, anger and injustice was overwhelming.

After the divorce my father was hit by a torrent of misfortune. He developed a duodenal ulcer and required a partial gastrectomy, which was the standard treatment at the time. It turned him into a dietary cripple. Then he caught the Adam curse of lung tuberculosis, which is often a complication of ulcers. He spent three years in and out of a chest sanatorium. That finished him as a doctor. He lost his practice, his house and what little money he had. He remarried and retired to a village on Dartmoor and a quiet life of walks, books and letters.

These events had a deep effect on me. I did not know what adultery was, but I vowed that when I married it would be for life. I would do everything possible to avoid my parents' mistakes. I would know when things went wrong and would say sorry and do whatever was necessary, even if I were not at fault. My philosophy of marriage was formed at an early age.

I was also deeply affected by my father's illness and forced retirement. Time and again I heard him blame overwork and a lack of support in the NHS for them, as well as poor medical treatment. If that were the price of becoming a doctor and looking after sick people, you could keep it. Medicine seemed a cruel mistress.

4

Epsom, Oxford and Fleet Street

When it learned of my father's plight, Epsom College, a boys' public school in Surrey, came to our rescue in a most generous way. The College was founded in the 19th century for the sons of doctors, and it granted me a scholarship with free tuition and boarding. Its motto is *Deo Non Fortuna*, which translates as 'By God not by Fortune.' Most of us rendered it as, 'By God, no luck!' Having no religious spark as yet, I found it easier to ascribe my fortune to luck not Providence.

My family tree

At Epsom it was expected that boys would follow their fathers into medicine. My family tree was laden with sawbones. They perched like vultures on the branches. On the Adam side we had four GPs and an eye surgeon. On my mother's side, albeit by marriage, we had a principal assistant-secretary of the

British Medical Association and a professor of respiratory medicine, whatever that meant. We also had a Victorian ancestor called William Octavius Garstin, an undertaker who conducted the first legal cremation in Britain at Woking in 1885. And a cousin of mine established the infamous London Dungeons, a celebration of gore. That record may seem impressive, but it was a comet that was fizzling out. In my generation only the professor's daughter and I became doctors.

Fortunately, my sister Ruth also received help with her education in the form of a bursary from St. Helen's Girls' School in Northwood. She started young and was very happy there. Unlike me she had no difficulty in deciding her future and went on to train in orthoptics at Moorfields Hospital.

* * *

The careers master at Epsom was a science graduate who did not seem entirely clear about his role. He hitched his bottom over a radiator and surveyed a roomful of fifth formers which included me.

'How many of you know what you're going to do after leaving Epsom?' A forest of hands shot up. They were the boys whose smirks said, 'my-dad's-a-doctor' or 'my-old-man-owns-a-business.'

'You lot can leave if you've got no questions.' There was a clatter of feet. He turned to the rest of us. 'It's not my job to influence you unduly but most of you haven't even chosen your A-levels yet. I'm here to point out the advantages of certain paths you may take. Let's start with the basics.'

I was one of those who had not yet made a choice. I expected him to talk about the merits of banking or joining the army. Instead he lectured us on the British public school system and how the Victorians over-rewarded Latin and Greek at the expense of the sciences. Apparently that was why we had fallen behind the Germans and Americans, who were now the richest nations on earth.

'You have no idea how fortunate you are! Epsom is only twenty miles from London, and London has the best twelve medical schools in England.' He reminded us that the College had a medical sixth form and a medical society. Apparently that made us unique. Our governors were distinguished medical men, peers and knights of the realm with entire alphabets after their names. Most importantly, we played rugby against the teaching hospitals and promising players were not forgotten.

I do not recall if Epsom's Masonic Lodge was mentioned. Its tentacles stretched throughout the medical world and offered other outrageous advantages. But at our age we were not expected to know about freemasonry.

The message was clear. When it came to getting a place at a medical school, Epsom College had the edge over its competitors. We did not have to grub around the provinces or the Celtic fringe. We had London sewn up.

Thus, during my six and a half years at Epsom there was every opportunity to choose medicine as a career. I frequently considered it but did not take it. One reason was that from an early age I was torn between science and the humanities; I was competent at both but found it hard to decide which to follow. The other reason, of course, was my father's misfortunes.

When my contemporaries left Epsom for the medical schools, I went up to Merton College in Oxford to read history. The three years I spent there were a glorious experience of spacious living, a term which meant that we played conspicuously harder than we worked. Some played sports, some played musical instruments and others just played. Our leisure hours were filled with parties, theatricals, debates, punting and drinking beer. None of us had much money, but that did not matter much.

On the 5th of November in my third year a noisy party was in progress on my staircase. I intended to look in for a drink before going off to see the fireworks. But I found more than fireworks that night. A stunning young lady caught my eye. She was in a black dress and nonchalantly smoking a black

Sobranie cigarette in an ebony holder. She confessed a passion for Wagner. I was intrigued.

'Which college are you at?'

'I'm not at the university. I work for Arthur Guinness in its regional office.'

'But haven't I seen you at lectures?'

'Yes, I borrow a gown and slip in when there's something good on.'

She also enjoyed undergraduate parties. Her name was Jacqui Maw, and she came from Cheltenham. Pretty soon we fell in love and became an item. Despite this and other distractions, I managed to get a decent second-class degree in history.

Regrettably, at this impressionable stage of my life, there was no older man to whom I could look for spiritual guidance. I was sceptical about religion, but I was not incurious, and I enjoyed a good debate. I loved my father, and I looked up to him, but he did not encourage spiritual discussion. Conversely, my mother was intensely spiritual and pressed her beliefs on me, urging me to attend whatever church she was attending. But her faith was so mixed up with bitterness about the divorce that I wanted no part of it. I had come to terms with the divorce and with Edna, my father's second wife, who was a very caring person and looked after him well. The last thing I wanted was for old wounds to be reopened.

There were family friends whom I admired but none had a faith about which they would talk. My tutors at Oxford were brilliant men but unforthcoming. One was Conrad Russell, the son of Lord Bertrand Russell, Britain's leading philosopher of the 20th century and an aggressive atheist. Trying to talk to him did me no good.

The chaplain at Merton College was a different sort. He took the freshmen aside during their first week and spoke seriously to them. 'If all you get out of Oxford is three years of pleasure and a degree, it will be a tragedy in your life.' I warmed to him, but within the year he had a heart attack and died.

* * *

For most students a degree in modern history was simply a passport to their first job. Few maintained an interest in the subject unless they intended to teach it. But history turned out to be an excellent preparation for journalism and for medicine, both of which I practised later. Studying a historical topic, writing an in-depth article, and taking a clinical history have much in common.

Let me explain that statement. In each situation you sift the grain from the chaff and form a theory of what has happened. In history it is your thesis, in journalism your headline and in medicine your diagnosis. In medicine every illness is a story and after you have heard it you perform a physical examination and test your diagnostic thoughts with deductive logic and tests. And you draw on your experiences of similar cases.

As part of the Oxford history course, we were expected to study a special period in detail. I chose the Peasants' Revolt of 1381. For two years I laboured over the original sources which were written in mediaeval French, Latin and Middle English. They were a nightmare to interpret, being full of ambiguities, fiction and propaganda. The experience later proved invaluable in sorting out patients' histories.

History also taught me how to write competently. While at Oxford I enjoyed some success in writing articles for local newspapers, and that helped me to get a position with *The Times* of London. I worked as a feature writer and editorial assistant on *The Times Review of Industry and Technology*, a monthly publication which has long since vanished. In its day it was well regarded in the business world and aspired to be another *Fortune* magazine. When the opportunity arose, I contributed to the daily paper.

A job on a prestigious paper in London in the Swinging Sixties was a merry-go-round. We rode it joyously while people in industry and business vied for our attention. There were endless press conferences, and outings that ranged from motor shows to fashion shows, and from factory openings to ship launches. The hospitality was lavish and one rarely paid for lunch.

It was the era of linotype printing. We typed our copy on manual Remington machines and passed it to the compositors who worked in the printing foundry. It came back two days later as galley proofs; strips of printed text a column wide and several feet long, like toilet paper without the perforations.

Overnight our office resembled a children's party in an arts and crafts centre. Red crayons, scissors, rulers and brushes lay everywhere, and the pungent smell of cow gum filled the air. The galley proofs were measured, cut into exact lengths, and stuck onto a backing of card. *Voila!* A page began to emerge.

Titles, headings, photographs and charts were added, and the text was unstuck and reattached to fit around them. This part had to be done with great care, since later changes cost money. Finally, the made-up pages were sent to the compositors and came back as page proofs. Linotype was thus a clumsy, time-consuming process and liable to errors. It gave way in the 1970s to computer-controlled phototypesetting. This was faster and cheaper and had none of the hazards of molten lead and asbestos.

But the excitement of the printing compensated for a lot. *The Times Review* was printed in the small hours after the daily paper went to bed. The sight of the lead being poured into the crucibles, the crashing of the majestic presses and the thrill of seeing the journals coming off the line was heady stuff.

Of course, there was far more to the job than gum and scissors. I liked the variety of technical journalism and the challenge of turning complex technical ideas into English that people could understand. But I also discovered that a novice in journalism depends heavily on his sources and that can be uncomfortable when people mislead you for their own ends. I dreamed of being not just a reporter but a correspondent, an expert in a field of my choosing. That would require specialized knowledge and experience which would take years to acquire.

* * *

Gradually the champagne life turned flat. There was too much pressure from public relations men and press officers, and a surfeit of rich food and late nights. I put on weight and acquired a taste for whisky. The long hours dulled my senses and even my relationship with Jacqui. She had come to London and was working as a secretary for a law firm in Lincoln's Inn, but I sensed that we were drifting apart.

On a press trip to a factory, I wrote some verses which I titled *Gentlemen of the Press* and which conveyed my sense of disillusionment:

> *It's nearly four and still*
> *We loll in the aftermath of luncheon,*
> *Mouths stale, drinks half finished.*
> *The dead dull voice drones on*
> *With facts, figures and projections.*
> *Time crawls by and now the only question is,*
> *Can we catch the ten past five?*

Back in the office I took stock of my situation. All the journalists in Fleet Street whom I admired had worked in their respective fields. The best defence correspondents were ex-servicemen, the best legal correspondents were lawyers, and the best shipping correspondents had worked in the shipping industry.

Out of that observation was born an idea which, in view of my previous aversion, seemed preposterous but which grew increasingly attractive as I considered it. Why not make a career in medical journalism? In those days few doctors worked in journalism. Few even deigned to talk to the press. As late as 1974 Dr David Devlin dared to write an article under his own name and was hauled before the General Medical Council for self-advertising.

So I hatched a plan to read medicine in order to become a medical correspondent. As I weighed the pros and cons of the matter, a small incident encouraged me. On *The Times Review* we had a medical contributor, an elderly doctor in Hampshire whom none of us ever met. He wrote his monthly pieces in ink and sent them in by post. His writing was a spidery scrawl that was barely legible. Sorting out the tangle was my job.

I begged the editor to drop him, but the snag was that he had been personal physician to Lord Astor who owned *The Times,* and he would not hear of it. One month the doctor's writing was so bad that I scrapped it and wrote a piece on Britain's mass chest x-ray programme. Nobody spotted the substitution, not even the doctor who was paid for my efforts. Presumably he did not check our pages.

I took to filling the medical column on a regular basis. Thus I moved seamlessly into medical journalism in a small way. It felt more worthwhile than much of the other stuff that I was writing, and I enjoyed the challenge.

When I announced my intention to change horses and go to medical school, there was a chorus of protests from my family. 'It's too late – you can't do that now! Ridiculous! – you're committed to journalism. Brazen! – you already have a degree at public expense. Heartless! – you're engaged to be married. What about Jacqui?'

My Epsom pals had by now qualified as doctors, and they took bets on how long it would take before I dropped by the wayside, if indeed I ever got started. Only Jacqui supported me, and of her own volition she changed jobs to work as a secretary in a large hospital in Bloomsbury. I took that as an encouragement to press on. Having made the decision, I was tempted to continue at *The Times* for a bit longer to save some money. But it would not be easy to return to full time education at twenty-four, and I might lose heart.

My editor took a cynical view, like most journalists. When he heard of my intention he said: 'It's a better job of course. Doctors earn more than we do.' He was right and I was not unaware of the prizes. All this goes to show what a callow and happy-go-lucky young man I was.

There is a Scottish saying, 'There are two reasons for doing something: a good reason and the real reason.' When people asked me why on earth I was switching to medicine, I gave the stock reason which could not be questioned, 'to help people.' But the truth was that I simply wanted to be a successful writer. Medicine was not my first choice of career. I had no thirst for scientific knowledge or an urge to find the cure for Alzheimer's disease. I had no great empathy for sick people and their problems.

Nor did I have to struggle to win a place at medical school against astronomical odds, as young people do today. If that had been the case, I would not have persevered.

In a cavalier manner I told Jacqui to put our engagement on hold and sped off to Epsom College to find a back door into medicine. I sought out my former housemaster, Rex Goddard, for whom I had a great affection. He quizzed me about my motives over several cups of tea and announced, 'I'll see what can be done. You're taking on a huge task, you know, and the hardest part will be getting in.'

5

Medical Starting Line

And so it was that one afternoon in the summer of 1963, I found myself in the offices of the Middlesex Hospital Medical School, waiting nervously to be interviewed by the Windy Knight (more on him below). The windows were open and through them I could hear the rumble of London's traffic. Sunlight glinted on the portraits of bewhiskered Victorian physicians which hung on the walls. They looked serene and superior, as if dismissive of this intruder from Grubb Street.

The school secretary, Miss Eileen Walton, was a delightful lady who did her best to put me at ease. She gave me a cup of tea and the latest copy of the school prospectus. I flicked the pages and read what I already knew: 'The Middlesex Hospital Medical School was established in 1825 by Sir Charles Bell. The Hospital was founded sixty years earlier to care for the poor and the lame who poured into London ...'

'He won't be long,' said Miss Walton reassuringly. 'He has a clinic at two. Would you like another cup?'

As I sipped from it, the spoon trembled slightly in the saucer. In my job on *The Times* I interviewed high powered businessmen and enjoyed putting awkward questions to them. Now the boot was on the other foot, and I was the one about to be roasted. The Windy Knight was Professor Sir Brian Windeyer, a tough Australian cancer specialist of international reputation. He had been appointed as radium officer at the Middlesex in 1931 when radiotherapy was in its infancy and a physically dangerous occupation. He had championed it for thirty years and climbed to the pinnacle. His next job would be Vice-Chancellor of London University.

He was burly, bulbous-nosed and bespectacled, and he sat like Moses in the seat of judgment. His face said, 'I am a man with whom you do not mess.' He looked me up and down and read my references. His opening question revealed what he thought of my application.

'So Mr Adam, you have an Oxford degree and a job. Why abandon a perfectly good career?' My discussions with Rex Goddard had prepared me for that, but not for the grilling that followed. Why had I not chosen medicine earlier? Why choose it now? Did I have any idea what I'd be letting myself in for? Did a man of my age really expect to achieve three A-levels in the sciences in eight months?

My answers sounded lame. Sir Brian grunted and polished his spectacles. The day was going badly. Suddenly I was relieved that I had not given in my notice to *The Times*.

Then something curious happened. The door opened, Miss Walton entered and whispered in Sir Brian's ear. He did the smallest double take and looked even more severe. But something had changed in the unseen realms. He pursed his lips and changed tack.

'What's your record in rugby? Did you play for Oxford? No? A pity. Your college perhaps?'

Finally he sighed, 'Very well, Adam. It's July and a new term starts in eight weeks. Can you get yourself together by then?'

And that, unbelievably, was how things were done in that era. There was no examination and no demand for triple-star A-levels or a grandiose personal statement. I did not have to show work experience in an abattoir or a leper colony.

All that a man needed was evidence that he was not a complete idiot and preferably had some sporting prowess. It helped if a relative had studied at the medical school in question. The grandfather of my friend Julian Turner studied with Sir Gordon Gordon-Taylor, a surgeon who was legendary at the Middlesex. The association secured Julian an interview with the great man and opened the door. This was despite the fact that Sir Gordon was well-retired from the hospital and the interview took place in Harley Street.

Let me return to my interview and Miss Walton. To this day I do not know what she whispered in the ear of the dean, but I imagine it was a detail that had escaped him, like a hint from a Middlesex surgeon who was an Old Epsomian. Rex Goddard had played his part behind the scenes. The old boy network was like the law of the Medes and the Persians; it could not be set aside.

And so I started First MB, which was the equivalent of three science A-levels, at the Middlesex Hospital Medical School on a grant of £5 a week and the sofa bed of a friend from Fleet Street days.

* * *

London in the 1960s had a glut of teaching hospitals. A dozen were crammed into a few square miles where they competed for patients, staff and money. They were inordinately jealous of their reputations, and most would not accept applicants who did not have a science background. The Middlesex was one of the few exceptions.

I fell in love with the place at first sight. Like Merton College it was a friendly, compact world. You soon got to know everyone who was of any importance. Patients loved the hospital because of its friendly ethos, which one historian described as 'much more than mere efficiency.'

It lay between Mortimer Street and Cleveland Street in London's West End and was surrounded by a warren of sweatshops that served the clothing, hat and fur industries. In 1963 many of them had been replaced by lock-up businesses and offices.

The medical school had grown alongside the hospital until it was squeezed out of the nest, but it remained within walking distance along back streets. It graduated no more than seventy doctors each year, but who cared? St. George's graduated only thirty.

At our induction ceremony in the Edward Lewis Theatre, we were treated to what we called 'the parade of the worthies,' the teaching staff in full academic regalia. We were welcomed with the words, 'You are now all Middlesex men and women.' Our youthful bosoms swelled. Maybe the salutation did not carry the resonance of 'Bart's or 'Tommy's men and women,' but it was character that counted, and we had plenty of that.

The first term was like trying to drink water from a fire hose. I gasped for breath under a torrent of facts, figures and theories. I struggled to absorb the information without being washed away.

Struggling with science

Most of my classmates were bright-eyed teenagers from school and six years my junior. I wrestled with scientific principles and logic, but they took easily to them. There were classes on medical statistics, and we were told to buy slide rules, but I never got the hang of mine. Laptops and notepads were many years in the future; the only occasion the word 'digital' was used was to refer to a rectal examination.

I also had to adjust to a big change in status and income. Until we knew each other better, my new friends regarded me as a kind of middle-aged drop-out. I put up with much good-natured ribbing.

As the first term finished, the pressure began to ease and I was drawn into the Christmas festivities. *The Manic Depressives* (the students' concert party) had high standards. The rehearsals were endless and soon I was neglecting Jacqui shamefully. But then a day came that changed our lives forever.

I remember it as clearly as if it were yesterday. During a noisy musical rehearsal I telephoned Jacqui from backstage to make a lame excuse for not seeing her. I thoughtlessly called her 'Honey', an endearment which she detested. (I never did it again.)

A bombshell exploded. 'Don't call me that!' she snapped. 'It's trivial and insincere!' Then she burst into huge sobs.

'Darling, what on earth is the matter?'

The band was playing the closing chorus, fifty feet away. *'The lights are going down all over London Town ...'*

I strained to hear her small voice through the racket. 'Can't you guess? Can't you see? I'm five months pregnant.'

'Wha-at?' ...

'So buenas noches, auf wiedersehen...'

Five months? How on earth had she reached to this point? How had I not noticed? How had *nobody* noticed? Surely her flatmates, or one of our friends... How could I have been so clueless?

Now the reason for Jacqui's ambivalence was clear. She'd been almost the only person to encourage me in my plan to take up medicine, and without her unwavering support I might never have done so. On the other hand she frequently implored, 'Darling, are you sure about this? You have to be completely sure.'

Through the sobs she said, 'I wouldn't t-tell until you c-completed a term. I wouldn't be the one to stop you. Now you have a chance to continue and become a d-doctor.' She had no idea of how I would react to news of the pregnancy.

And what was my reaction? At first, sheer panic. I could only see shame and disaster ahead. In 1963 the sexual revolution had hardly started, and the prevailing attitude was practical rather than puritan. 'Be good,' it said, 'but if you can't be good don't be stupid and don't get caught.'

I went round to her flat immediately. I was shaking like a leaf when I boarded a bus in Oxford Street, but by Hyde Park

Corner my nerves had steadied. By the time I arrived in South Kensington, fear had given way to excitement at the prospect of becoming a father. I knew what must happen next, even if it meant giving up medicine.

It was a tearful but happy reunion; neither of us doubted the love and sincerity of the other and we hastened to make plans for a quick wedding.

But first we had to tell our parents and I leave to your imagination the embarrassment we went through as an unmarried couple. After the initial shock they rallied round and drove up from their homes in Devon and Gloucestershire for the wedding. It took place on a cold morning in Christmas week at St Mary the Boltons in Kensington. At the modest reception, my father read out a spoof weather forecast. He spoke of a deep depression centred on London which spread to the west of England.

'Chilly conditions and poor reception were expected in these areas. Stormy atmospherics were minimal and reactions moderate and mainly fair. Further outlook: a little bit of sunshine on the way.' I loved him for that.

Our slender budget allowed only a two-night honeymoon in Brighton. My mother recommended a small hotel which she knew. 'It's just off the sea front. The owners are lovely and there's a nice fire in the lounge.' I looked up the telephone number. My voice shook at the novelty of making a booking for Mr and Mrs Adam.

At midnight on our wedding day, Jacqui and I arrived at Brighton railway station, completely exhausted. I gave a taxi driver the name of the hotel. He raised an eyebrow. 'Are you sure?' it seemed to say.

I missed the hint, and the result was that we found ourselves in budget lodgings for casual labourers. My mother got the name wrong. The Alexander Hotel had become the Hotel Alexis or something like it and we were shown a room which contained eight beds, all fortunately empty at the time. We endured one night and moved on. The highlight of the honeymoon was a mystery coach tour to Ditchling Beacon in the rain.

At the start of the second term, I stood again before Sir Brian's desk to report my change of circumstances. This time he did not invite me to sit. He glowered like a Victorian householder confronting a pregnant maidservant.

'Adam, you're a bloody fool!'

'Indeed, sir,'

'You should never have started. You'll have to leave.'

My throat went dry. 'Do you mean I'm expelled?'

'I've seen better men than you broken this way. You'll never qualify.'

'Sir, there are a dozen married students in the school. They seem to do alright.'

'They're in the clinical years and their records are clean. Your situation is different.'

I was close to panic. 'Sir, am I being expelled?'

'No. But just pack your things and leave!'

The ground declined to swallow me up. I left muttering, 'I'll think about it."

6

Carrying on Regardless

No doubt Sir Brian had my interests and those of the medical school at heart and he only told me what others were saying. But his response was so ungentle that it backfired. I was angry and upset. My ambition was to read medicine, and I had made a significant sacrifice for it.

That evening Jacqui and I talked deep into the night. She too had made sacrifices and she encouraged me to carry on. 'Darling, the trouble is that Sir Brian doesn't know you. You are not the usual kind of medical student. I know that because I've met the others.'

I grew more determined than ever. Suddenly a medical degree changed, with Jacqui's participation, from a private ambition to a joint adventure. Now, as Mills and Boon might put it, we were two young people going forward hand in hand.

Whenever I look back on those years, as I have at length when writing this book, I realise just how much I owe Jacqui. The dean could only see the pressures and divided loyalties that a married student must go through. But the love, loyalty and encouragement I received from my wife, the stability of our family life and the self-discipline that I learned as husband and provider more than compensated for the difficulties.

Here I should say a word about my fellow students, to whom also I owe a great deal. In *Pickwick Papers,* Bob Sawyer's landlady describes medical students as, 'a parcel of lazy, idle fellars that are always smoking and drinking, and lounging ... a parcel of young cutters and carvers of live people's bodies that disgraces the lodgings.'

I agree that a fair amount of smoking, drinking and lounging went on, but we were no disgrace. We were a good deal more purposeful than Richard Gordon's roguish characters in *Doctor in the House*. We were from private and state schools, brainy and average, bookish and sporty. Medicine was still the domain of male students (less than ten per cent were women) which brings me to a delicate point. When writing about students and doctors it will be tiresome constantly to write 'he or she did so-and-so.' So, with apologies to the gentler sex, I shall use the male gender and hope to be forgiven.

Nor must I forget the older students. As I have mentioned, most of my intake was fresh from school but a few were several years older and had seen something of life. We formed a circle within the circle. It included a former colonial administrator, a male nurse, an Oxford linguist, a master mariner, and a successful businessman. One of our lecturers was invited to dine at the home of the businessman and was astonished when a butler opened the door.

Medical schools in those days regarded their students as feral; they needed breaking in before they were allowed on the wards. The first half of the six-year course was spent learning theory in classrooms and laboratories. That meant that when we reached the wards we had no clinical skills and no idea of how to relate to patients. We were like men who had been imprisoned in a monastery and were suddenly released into a harem.

* * *

In the summer of 1964 my class passed First MB and started MB Part II. We progressed from dogfish to human anatomy, which the medical school took very seriously. We learned it the old way, by the laborious and systematic dissection of a corpse. The school's founder Sir Charles Bell was a famous surgeon-anatomist, and there would be no dodging the lectures and dissecting sessions.

We were introduced to Eldred Walls, the Glaswegian-born professor of anatomy. He cut an impressive Edwardian figure in his black coat, striped trousers and stiff collar. He was of cadaveric build, being tall and fleshless, which added to his professional credibility.

In the lecture hall Professor Walls was a master of rhetoric, particularly when describing the external sphincter of the anus, about which he had written learned papers. The anus was, as everybody knew, a highly sensitive area and we all had an interest in ensuring that it functioned correctly. That fact alone commanded respect for his work. Even consultant surgeons (and he had taught anatomy to many) were in awe of him.

He prided himself on his teaching and hated being interrupted. He was something of an orator and you do not interrupt orators when they are in full flow.

A very sensitive subject

Eldred was also a veritable Leonardo at the blackboard. From time to time he stood back to admire his work and exclaimed, '*Gray's Anatomy* couldn't do better than that!' He was a brilliant stippler with coloured chalks. Indeed, he could have stippled for Scotland.

Eldred insisted that the same respect be paid to the dead as to live patients. 'Ladies and gentlemen, you will be properly dressed at all times in the dissection room. Gentlemen will note that includes the wearing of a necktie.'

It was a ludicrous instruction, since a tie inevitably flopped out at some point into the dissection and was ruined.

(For some reason tie pins were considered decadent.) Gynaecologists face a similar problem when they place ladies on their backs with legs hoisted up in stirrups, in the lithotomy position. In my day sensible gynaecologists wore bow ties. Today most of them go tieless.

Nevertheless at our first class we arrived in neck ties and crisp white coats, clutching our scalpels, probes and tweezers wrapped in a canvas roll.

The dissecting room was on the fifth floor of the medical school, away from prying eyes. When you entered, the smell of embalming fluid hit you like a blast. It was a mixture of formaldehyde, phenol and glycerol that brought tears to the eyes.

A row of tables covered by sheets awaited us and beneath the sheets were a row of mounds. A foot stuck out from one of them with a label attached to the large toe.

I had never seen a dead body and remember praying, 'Please God, if anyone faints don't let it be me.' When the sheets were removed, we stared at the waxen faces and someone breathed, 'They don't look real, do they?' Everyone relaxed; the first hurdle was passed.

We were assigned to the bodies in groups of eight, two to an arm and two to a leg. The aforementioned Julian Turner was my dissecting partner on the opposite leg. During months of slicing, probing and removing, we lost our sense of awe. The bodies came to resemble scarecrows and shrank in size as we discarded what we dissected. Our white coats turned greasy yellow.

The anatomy demonstrators were young trainee surgeons and they too had lost any sense of awe they once possessed. They had no time for philosophizing and grilled us ferociously to expose the boundaries of our ignorance.

Today anatomy has been squeezed into the margins of the medical curriculum. Many students never enter a dissection room or a mortuary, and I have known young doctors start their first hospital job without having seen a dead body.

They learn whatever is prescribed from live CCTV demonstrations, videos and handling specimens that have been plastinated, a process that removes water and fat from human tissues and replaces them with synthetic resins. The specimens do not smell or decay.

In fairness, few doctors need a detailed knowledge of anatomy. The subject was unquestionably overtaught in my day and we soon forgot most of what we learned. We used flash cards, acronyms and mnemonics to scrape through the examinations. I still remember the structures which pass through the *foramen ovale* (an opening in the base of the skull) and the wandering course of the lingual nerve:

> *The lingual nerve, it took a swerve around the hyoglossus.*
> *Said Walton's Duct well I'll be f****d!*
> *The blighter double-crossed us.*

You get the picture. There were many such rhymes, most of them unrepeatable in polite society.

Even as a student I found something profound in spending time with the dead. I soon overcame my revulsion at the sight of blood and raw tissues. Handling wet anatomy and seeing the effects of disease focused one's mind on the fragility of life. For me it was a reverential experience, and the vapour of embalming fluid was its incense. My attraction to pathology started at this point.

In parallel with anatomy we learned physiology, which is the normal working of the human body. In one experiment, we had to measure each other's blood pressures, heart rate and urine output before and after drinking large amounts of coffee. We tended to swig gallons of the stuff anyway while swotting for exams, so the lab results were valueless.

Charles Shaw occupied lodgings in Nassau Street with three friends and he took physiology seriously. He discovered a simpler and cheaper way to stay awake than swilling coffee; he munched dry coffee beans through the night. They left him quaking like a leaf from caffeine overdose, but they did the trick and he never failed an exam.

On another occasion that particular group were intrigued to learn that cow flatus contains a mixture of methane gas and hydrogen, and that it can sometimes be set alight. One of them decided, in the interest of science, to put human flatus to the test. It ignited so successfully that he needed to be treated in the Casualty Department for singeing his nether parts.

* * *

All medical students experience financial difficulties, some of them permanently. In the summer we took jobs to balance the books. One of my friends was a dustman, another worked in a brick factory, and another sold wallpaper off the back of a lorry. Few of us tried nursing, which was a pity. We would have benefitted from acquiring some of the compassion and dedication of our sister profession.

Julian Turner was an exception; he was a nursing aide during his vacations. He wrote, 'I learned to pay more respect to the lower ranks (i.e. the nurses) than the pompous consultants. A builder was admitted with shaking episodes which the consultant physician said were hysteria. A petite first-year Indian nurse muttered, "I think this is tetanus." Her diagnosis proved correct, but the doctor never admitted his error.'

My own life was a continual cash flow crisis. My grant as a single student was five pounds a week (the equivalent of £80 today), and it was not increased when I married. There was no way it would support two adults and a baby. However, my time in Fleet Street saved us. I contacted the editor of a medical weekly for GPs, gave him my hard luck story and he accepted my pitch for a feature article.

Other commissions followed, and I was soon hammering out articles every weekend in our flat in North London. Medical conferences, public lectures, trade fairs, book reviews, rugby cuppers ... all was grist to my typewriter. I became a founder member of the Medical Journalists Association, which was birthed in Ye Olde Cheshire Cheese pub on Fleet Street.

In addition to writing, I did some male modelling. Nothing hedonistic, you understand, just hats and sweaters. I also performed cabaret for cash with a group of older students.

Our high-water mark was performing at the summer ball of the Wentworth Golf Club.

Jacqui found part-time secretarial work with John Creightmore, a GP in private practice in Kensington. He was a Bart's man, who became our great friend and godfather to our son Rob. John was an eligible bachelor; he was duty doctor to the Royal Ballet Company and to Covent Garden Opera House and he once escorted Princess Anne to a performance of *No Sex Please, We're British*. He kept a jar containing Margot Fonteyn's pickled appendix on his mantelpiece.

He bequeathed me Betty, a half-skeleton who was a relic of his student days. She was geriatric when John bought her and must be over 150 years old now. She saw me through my undergraduate exams and helped me qualify as a pathologist. I used her to test my children and grandchildren for any interest in medicine, but she struck no sparks there. Nonetheless she remains a valued heirloom. She lives in a wooden box in our attic.

In the same way my friend Nick Mumford had a skull called Toby which, after it had seen him through medicine, ended up in his parents' home. When Jehovah's Witnesses rang the doorbell, they were greeted by Mr Mumford senior with Toby under his arm. Their calls tended to be brief.

As soon as Rob arrived, we put him to work modelling baby clothes and blankets with the agency which employed me. Thus the whole family was on a payroll. To keep the flow of articles going, I sometimes had to miss classes in order to attend newsworthy events. My chums, who knew my situation, gathered round. They lent me their lecture notes, explained the finer points, and generally helped me not to fall behind. When Rob was older, they baby-sat so that Jacqui and I got an occasional night out at the cinema.

* * *

One writing commission sticks in my mind because it was a foretaste of work I would do in the RAF. In the mid-1960s an organization called the British Medical Pilots Association held a 'fly-in' in Portsmouth. I reported the event for the medical press and still have the fading newspaper cuttings. About sixty doctors attended, including a good number who owned their own planes. They flew into Portsmouth airport in Cessnas and Pipers, and so did I with a doctor friend who hired a Cessna for the occasion.

The main speaker at the conference was Wing Commander Peter Stevens, an RAF consultant in aviation pathology whom I came to know well in later years. I admired his quiet scholarly approach to unsavoury topics. He introduced the first session by saying, 'Ladies and gentlemen, we know that the UK is facing an epidemic in fatal accidents in light aircraft. The figures are alarmingly high. It's partly the fault of the pilots and partly that of their medical examiners. Government action is long overdue in this area.'

There were rumbles of agreement from the audience. They were pilots who knew about aviation medicine first hand, whereas most medical examiners were GPs without any training or experience. Annual medical exams were a lucrative pond in which to fish and it attracted anglers of all kinds.

Peter reported the results of his research. By comparing the official accident reports with the pilots' NHS medical records and post-mortem findings, it was clear that many pilots were behaving irresponsibly. During their annual medical examinations they would say and do anything to beat the system and stay airborne. They concealed symptoms of heart disease, migraine, epilepsy and eye complaints. They misled the examiners about their alcohol consumption and medications. A few even used recreational drugs and did not admit it. The facts only came to light in the tests on their blood and urine which were taken post-mortem.

On the other side, the examiners took far too much on trust. They failed to ask the right questions. They ignored tell tale signs of alcohol and drug abuse in pilots and seemed unaware of the effect of even mild usage upon their performance. Most had never been up in a light aircraft, let alone piloted one. The thresholds of safety which they employed were far too low.

Peter had a collection of slides to illustrate fatal crashes. With each one the room seemed to grow more and more chilly. Members' wives left and showed no sign of returning. From a distance I eyed the man who had flown me down in a hired airplane. He was a nice enough chap, but his piloting and map skills were rusty, and he had needed two attempts to land at Portsmouth. When the conference ended, I made my excuses and took a train back to London.

Happily the story had a positive sequel. The Ministry of Aviation formed a panel of medical experts trained in aviation medicine. They alone were authorized to perform the medical examination of all pilots and glider pilots in the UK. A new era in occupational medicine began and it has been a blessing to aviators ever since.

The second speaker also had a sobering effect on the company. He showed that medically qualified pilots in the USA were far less safe in the cockpit than non-medical ones. They were four times more likely to be killed in aircraft crashes. He described the fate of doctors who ignored safety warnings. Some took off in the face of bad weather, presumably believing they could soar above it. One man took off at night from an unlit airstrip relying on his car's headlights.

This attitude was known as the Icarus syndrome. Icarus was a figure in Greek mythology whose father crafted a set of wings out of feathers and wax. The boy was so thrilled to fly that he ignored his father's warnings and soared too close to the sun. The wax melted and he fell to his death. Thus Icarus describes an overweening self-confidence combined with a reckless attitude to danger. It is sometimes applied to ambitious politicians who crash and burn. Admittedly the warning was from across the Atlantic, but they say that what America does today the Brits do tomorrow.

* * *

Back in London I had to meet up with my course mentor, a biology lecturer called Ronald Withers.

'What were you doing in Portsmouth?' he asked, and he shook his head when I told him. 'Andy, you seem to be a freelance journalist who fits medicine into your spare time.'

To convince him that I was on target and would qualify, I told him about Dr Michael O'Donnell, a distinguished medical editor who was providing me with work. When he applied to a medical school in the 1940s he asked his interviewer, 'Would this school countenance the notion of a part-time medical student?' The answer was, 'Is there any other kind?'

I begged Mr Withers not to report me to the dean. He was a kindly man who knew my circumstances and he agreed to keep his concerns to himself, for the moment. 'Let's see how things work out,' he said.

7

Clerks and Dressers

At our final anatomy class, as we quit the lecture rooms for the wards, Professor Eldred Walls bade us farewell with these words: 'Ladies and gentlemen, always strive to preserve the high standards of the Middlesex Hospital. Deference and respect must be given and received at all levels.'

Someone nudged me from behind. 'That's you, Andy. He hasn't forgotten.'

It had happened, of course, during a Christmas concert. Dressed in a black jacket, wing collar and striped trousers identical to his own, I had impersonated Eldred lecturing on the innards of a toilet cistern. The lavatorial sound effects were particularly good and my Glaswegian accent was well-rehearsed. The piece went down well with everybody except Eldred. He did not speak to me for months. I felt a little uneasy, since he was tipped to be the next dean.

The concerts, of which I shall say more later, were a Fools' Holiday when jesters aped their masters and deference went out of the window. At other times deference was essential. The hospital administration was in the hands of a secretary-superintendent who was a retired brigadier-general; his next job would be as Master of the Royal Household. And the Matron, Miss Marjorie Marriott, was a benevolent despot who held the title of Lady Superintendent of Nurses. She ruled her realm with a firm sceptre.

We had over seventy consultants who enjoyed the status of Old Testament patriarchs. The older ones had been appointed in the 1930s and had distinguished war records. They held the power on the hospital's board of governors. The chairman was Lord Cobbold, who was the Lord Chamberlain and a former Governor of the Bank of England. The medical school council was chaired by another hereditary peer, Lord Astor of Hever. Blood did not come bluer.

Allow me to give you the flavour of a Monday morning in the 1960s, starting in the hospital forecourt. At around 8.00 a.m. the consultants would arrive in their Bentleys and Daimlers and park in their spaces. The registrars arrived an hour earlier in bicycle clips.

'Good morning, Mr Slack! Good morning, Professor Kekwick, sir!' The arrivals were saluted and greeted by the head porter, Mr William Webster. The hospital's liveried porters were the epitome of smartness in frock coats and brass-buttoned waistcoats. No less than twenty-nine of them were employed around the different departments. A favourite with the students was Phil Baker, who operated the elevator on the East Wing. 'I lift humanity to new heights,' was his boast. He was a former theatrical agent manager and greeted visitors with a line from Shakespeare or Noel Coward.

A polished board hung above the desk operated by the front hall porters. It displayed the consultants' names in gilt letters on panels. As they arrived, like the Orient Express drawing into Istanbul, their names were slid from the OUT to the IN-side of the board.

Four enormous oil paintings entitled *Acts of Mercy* dominated the front hall. Painted by Frederick Cayley Robinson in the early 1900s, they portrayed mothers, orphans, the sick and aged and the wounded. They epitomized the Middlesex's motto, *Miseris Succurrere Disco* ('I learn to help the wretched'). The pre-Raphaelite style was outmoded, but the pictures had a haunting appeal. One consultant wrote of them, 'My life was made happier by the presence of those paintings,' and another called them 'a daily pleasure and inspiration.' That's something you cannot say of a modern hospital foyer.

The days had gone when junior medical staff waited for their consultant in the front hall. Now they gathered upstairs on the ward. The ward sister prepared his coffee and biscuits while the house officer got the notes and x-rays together for the ward round. The entire team progressed around the beds in a time-honoured order. First the consultant in conversation with the senior registrar and the sister, and then the junior registrar followed by the senior house officer. The house physician (or surgeon) trailed a few yards behind.

The staff nurses fitted in somewhere after the registrars. In any dispute they would put the students to flight, but they deferred to the house officers. Their neatly starched hats gave them an air of pert efficiency and prevented straggling hairs. Why, I wonder, did today's cross-infection committees do away with them?

Weekly highlight

We medical students came last, like a gaggle of Soho waiters in short white bum-freezer jackets with a copy of *The British National Formulary* stuffed into a pocket. We rotated around the medical and surgical wards in 'firms'. Each firm was a group of eight students whose composition did not change, which was an excellent thing. When we were farmed out to other hospitals, the firm provided the continuity and stability in which we could learn, grow and support each other.

On the medical firms we were called 'clerks', because we made the initial examination of patients and entered our findings in the notes. On surgical firms we were called 'dressers', a term harking back to the days when students were responsible for bandaging wounds. The nurses knew far more about that sort of thing than the average student would ever learn.

The teaching round was the highlight of the week. The junior doctors stood back, and the students lined up around the bed.

We tried hard to look as though we were intimately acquainted with each case, but we also shuffled around to keep out of the consultant's line of sight.

Many are the stories about ward rounds: the repartee, the inspirational and the dismal teaching, the humiliations, the moments of terror and the lucky guesses. Some of them are true. I can vouch for one about Mr J.H.L. Ferguson. He was an excellent surgeon and a popular sub-dean, and I was a dresser on his firm.

He removed a gall bladder from a very obese lady. You must understand that gall bladders are good for little except forming stones, which makes them a surgeon's playground.

It was a difficult operation because of the patient's obesity and Mr Ferguson proudly presented her with a plastic pot filled with small yellow-green stones. On his ward round the next week, he paused in surprise.

'Mrs Davies, the number of gall stones in your pot has gone down.'

'Stones, doctor? Blimey I thought them was my medicine. I've been taking one every day.'

Fergie had a dry sense of humour. On another occasion he operated on a civil servant with odd-looking haemorrhoids. The scalpel slipped and he nicked his finger. Five weeks later he reported privately to Dr Duncan Catteral, the top man in Genito-Urinary Medicine, commonly known as the Clap and Pox Department.

Fergie had a painless ulcer on his index finger and enlarged lymph nodes in his armpit, a classic presentation of primary syphilis. Dr Catteral performed the appropriate tests and confirmed the presence of the spirochaetes which cause it. Happily, the infection responded well to penicillin and Fergie had no further problems, other than explaining things to his wife.

Most clinicians would have kept quiet about something like this but Fergie was not one to miss a teaching opportunity. The story was recounted with gusto in the hospital journal, of how he and his registrar searched the notes of dozens of patients, and how nobody had read the histopathology report which showed that the 'haemorrhoids' were actually syphilitic warts. The civil servant had recently contracted the disease as a result of his lifestyle. His contacts were traced and treated, and all ended well.

* * *

Our status as students was lowly but important, since we were responsible for taking blood specimens from the patients. 'Here come the vampires again!' they cried, when we hit the wards with our trays and trolleys. It was an old joke, and we did our best to raise a smile.

We practised puncturing each other's skin and the skin of oranges, but almost everything to do with blood-taking is learned on the job. Today professional phlebotomists are trained to do nothing but draw blood and they rarely fail.

No vein likes to be punctured. Some of them seem to have a premonition and collapse the instant you approach them. In obese patients they vanish into the fat, like earthworms evading a blackbird. Elderly ladies have veins as thin as gossamer. If you do not apply exactly the right amount of pressure when withdrawing the needle, you cause a spectacular bruise which persists for weeks as evidence of your clumsiness. And some patients are simply as bloodless as Martians.

When you have mastered the art of puncturing a vein to take out blood, you must then master cannulation, which is inserting a plastic tube into a vein so that fluids and drugs can be introduced through a drip. You do this using a far larger needle than the ones used to take blood. It is often an urgent procedure performed in the middle of the night when nobody is around to help.

Male students in those days had another role: surgical barber. In bygone days barbers lopped off arms and legs that had been shattered on a battlefield. In my day they shaved the torsos, legs and private parts of male patients on the eve of an operation. The nurses were not involved in these procedures, which were sometimes nipple-to-knee, but they did administer bed baths. Occasionally a male patient enjoyed his bed bath so much that a tent pole sprang up beneath the blanket. This was reduced by surgical spirit, liberally applied to a large cotton wool dressing.

The most popular medical firm at the Middlesex was the cardiology firm of Drs Walter Somerville and Richard Emmanuel, where we learned the clicks and murmurs of heart valves and a dozen different kinds of pulse. Walter Somerville was an Irish physician with film star looks. He drove a Mercedes sports car and always wore a red carnation in his buttonhole.

Once, for a laugh, we all turned up wearing carnations. Walter said not a word and we feared that we had offended him, so we resolved not to do it again. The next week he came with a box of the buttonholes and handed them out. 'Ladies and gentlemen, we can't have this! You are all in a state of undress.'

Today student firms have largely vanished, destroyed by European working time directives and bureaucratic interference. I regret their passing just as I regret the informal dress which students and doctors feel free to adopt nowadays. But I am a grumpy old man in this regard and there is no turning the clock back.

Every teaching hospital had a pub that was, in Richard Gordon's words, 'as much a part of the hospital as the main operating theatre.' Ours was the King and Queen in Foley Street which was run by a couple called Tom and Rose. They watched generations of teenagers develop into professional men and women and looked on them as the children they never had. Rose owned a Chihuahua which was no bigger than a lab rat. It fitted into a pint mug, and she lavished affection and potato crisps upon it. A student in a senior year called Robert Harvey once asked her for a Chihuahua sandwich and was thrown off the premises.

In the King and Queen, we celebrated our successes on the sports field and in examinations, romances and job hunting. We drowned our sorrows in Watney's Red Ale costing 7½ p a pint. If we were too rowdy and got chucked out, we went to the Cambridge in Newman Street, which no longer exists.

I say 'we', but as a married man I spent little time in pubs. I did however edit *The Middlesex Hospital Journal* and wrote scripts for the Christmas concerts. Even our rivals agreed that they were the best and most professional shows of any London medical school. That was partly because we had an auditorium that was as good as a West End theatre. Sir Edward Lewis, the chairman of Decca Recording and a prodigious benefactor of the Middlesex, donated it.

In the mid-1960s the show ran for eight nights but still could not meet the demand for 5,000 tickets. One reason was that the consultants loved to be made fun of. It was a badge of honour and they returned night after night with their families and friends to enjoy a hammering. As I have shown, Professor Walls was an exception. He did not appreciate the toilet sketch.

A later dean and historian of the medical school wrote, 'Many a member of staff has emerged from the auditorium after one of the shows asking, 'Do I really look like that?' or 'Do I have that habit?" Many of the caricatures were outrageous, but they all had the germ of truth and the best ones passed into legend. Some were vulgar, of course, in the tradition of the 1960's cult comedy *Carry on Doctor*. The great music hall comedian George Robey (who once appeared in charity concerts at the Middlesex) noted that there was nothing that the British public enjoy so much as a little vulgarity.

A lot of ingenuity went into finding names for the concerts. They were puns on better known titles, for example *Lady Chatterley's Liver, Great Expectorations* and *Beyond the Syringe*.

One title so offended the Matron that she banned the nurses from participating. This created a major crisis. Within a short time, posters appeared announcing that the concert had a new title: *The Name's the Same*. No one could object to that, and things went ahead as normal.

The scriptwriters' meetings were lengthy affairs which took place in smoke-filled rooms over a crate of beer. They went on into the small hours and often ground to a halt.

'Alright, so we've got the dean up a lamp post pursued by the brigadier who's wearing a pith helmet and a tutu. What happens next?'

Silence.

'Maybe the lamp post is outside Matron's bathroom window?'

Silence.

'If we want a laugh every 25 seconds and the concert lasts two hours, we need 288 jokes. How many so far?

'Three.'

'Four, if you count the one about the gynaecologist and the …'

'Three.'

The best script that I wrote was pinched by an unscrupulous member of the company. Some years after we had gone our ways, I was astonished to see it performed in a BBC variety show. I never tracked him down and shall not name him, but he was the concert producer, not more than five feet four inches tall and everybody knows who I mean.

Rehearsals for the Christmas concerts were time-consuming and caused me a memorable exam failure. In December 1966 I barely had time to turn up for the pharmacology papers. I was so poorly prepared that I could not have explained the difference between sulphonamides and snake oil.

The pharmacology professor was Franz Hobbiger, a brilliant Austrian scientist who lost a leg while fighting in Hitler's army. At the Middlesex he specialised in nerve gases, and he was a consultant at Porton Down, the oldest chemical warfare research station in the world. It was good to know that he was finally on our side, but he cut me no slack that day.

I sensed failure coming when he abandoned the clever stuff and asked something basic. 'Mr Adam, vot laxatives do you know?'

My mind was a blank, apart from croton oil. It is a bowel opener so ferocious that most civilized countries ban it. During World War II, the United States Navy added small amounts to the alcohol which powered torpedoes. It prevented sailors from drinking the stuff.

'Croton? Really? Vot dosage vould you prescribe?'

I took a wild guess. 'Thirty milligrams, sir.'

Hobbiger choked. 'My friend, that dose of croton oil vould blow the backside off an elephant!'

* * *

Once I started on the wards there was no time to continue with freelance writing, so Jacqui and her friend Barbara Johnson dreamed up a scheme to keep both our families afloat. It was a decorative hair bow, a cross between a cocktail hat and a Spanish mantilla. The girls fashioned them from velvet ribbons and copper wire. They mounted them on plastic combs with tubes of Bostik.

A cottage industry sprang up in our basement flat in Victoria. Spools of ribbons and wire lay everywhere as the girls cut, measured, spliced and glued. The finished bows were spread over the floors and chairs to dry. They seemed to giggle a lot over them. I suspected that they were high on Bostik, long before glue sniffing became fashionable.

Every month Barbara sallied forth with boxes of bows under her arm to tour the West End department stores. Harrods, Selfridges and Fortnum and Mason bought them, as did Niemann Marcus in the USA. Princess Margaret (the Queen's younger sister and a notable fashion setter) was seen wearing one in a night club. Jacqui and Barbara never became rich, but their efforts kept the wolf from the door for a little longer.

8

Taking the Queen's Shilling

Despite everybody's best efforts the debts mounted up. One day in 1966, when I was 27 years old, I came into the kitchen with a long face and sat down with Jacqui. 'Darling, I've been doing our accounts. I calculate that by the time I qualify – if all goes well, with no slip ups – we'll owe at least £1,500.'

'Can't we manage that?'

'That's two years salary for a house officer. It would take years to pay back.'

How curious such scruples seem today, when students are encouraged to borrow astronomical sums which everybody knows they may never repay. But my father's misfortunes had bred in me a loathing of debt.

Happily, a solution was at hand. If you passed the halfway exam in medicine it was assumed that you would pass the finishing post; you could apply to the Armed Forces for a cadetship. You received a junior officer's pay and allowances until you qualified and served your pre-registration year. Then you repaid the Queen with five years as a medical officer.

By now Professor Walls had replaced the Windy Knight as dean of the medical school and he did not approve of the recruiting scheme. 'You must see that it's a form of bribery, Mr Adam,' he told me in his sonorous Glaswegian voice. 'You are limiting your professional options and I fear that you may regret it.'

I had no qualms about serving in uniform. I narrowly missed doing two years National Service, but I had been a member of the Officers' Training Corps at Oxford. (It paid me to learn how to drive and obtain my driving licence for free.) I had done my homework and the medical branches of the Armed Forces had sound reputations. I set my sights on the Royal Air Force.

At an interview in Whitehall, a senior medical officer looked me up and down with the same lack of enthusiasm that Sir Brian Windeyer had displayed.

'So Adam, you're on the home straight. Why join the RAF?'

I gave the interviewer a noble speech about serving Queen and Country, passing over any sordid financial motive. I doubt that it fooled him. My Middlesex colleague Nick Mumford was asked the same question a few months later and replied, 'Sir, I'm married with a child. I need the cash to get my degree.'

'Indeed? Well, you'll have our answer shortly.'

Nick was surprised, a few days after the interview, to be offered a commission. He told me, 'I chanced my luck, rang up the officer and asked him why I had been accepted. He said, "Simple. You were the only candidate to tell the truth that day."'

I might just as well have played it straight like Nick, but nevertheless I was accepted. After a medical examination and other formalities, I received orders to report to an RAF station outside London to be commissioned. A dozen medical students were sworn in on that day. I was now Pilot Officer Adam. To buy myself out in the next seven years would cost £3,800, nearly £70,000 today. It was gratifying to see how much I had become worth overnight.

It took a morning to fill in the forms. At one point the flight sergeant who was supervising asked, 'Gents, the RAF needs to know what denomination you are.' We fell silent. 'If you're not sure, you're C of E.'

One man joked, 'Flight, if the Tory party is the Anglican Church at prayer, is the RAF the Anglicans at war?'

The flight sergeant eyed him blankly. 'Dunno about that sir. But if you're not C of E, you're an Arsie. And if you're not an Arsie, you're Odds and Sods.'

It took a moment to work out that Arsies were RCs, and the Odds and Sods were Other Denominations. The latter included agnostics, humanists, Jews and (for all we knew) Rastafarians. A visiting Methodist minister looked after them.

We hesitated. Our supervisor lowered his voice. 'Gents, the RAF doesn't give a brass monkey what you choose. It needs to know what funeral arrangements to make if you die on overseas service.'

C of E seemed the best option. After all, it does pretty good funerals.

* * *

My status as a pilot officer made a world of difference to our little family. I spent most of my uniform allowance on a second-hand car and we enjoyed an unseasonable holiday in Snowdonia in March. I joined the RAF Club in Piccadilly, whose dining room was a delight after the students' canteen and did wonders for my morale.

Now I could concentrate on my studies without having to earn money by writing. Most important of all, we were able to have a second child and not worry how to afford her. Our daughter Kate was born at the Middlesex Hospital in December 1967.

The title of a London University medical degree is MBBS (Bachelor of Medicine and Bachelor of Surgery). The course was six and a half years long and it was drawing to a close. It had been a journey of discovery not just about medicine but about our character, abilities and limitations. In the final year we were allowed to choose one great adventure for ourselves. This was the elective period, eight weeks to be spent anywhere in the world immersed in a different kind of medicine.

The elective did not contribute marks towards finals, so if your finances permitted you could indulge yourself. Florida and the Caribbean islands were popular, but you needed to apply well in advance. African mission hospitals were popular with the bolder spirits. There you stepped out of your comfort zone.

I did not fancy doctoring in the jungle or the bush and chose a month's attachment at the Luton and Dunstable Hospital. It had challenges of a different kind, being within a few hundred yards of the juggernauts that roared up and down the M1 motorway. It received a constant flow of accidents. In those days trauma was treated by orthopaedic surgeons and at the time I was interested in orthopaedics, or so I thought.

My time was divided between the Casualty Department (the term Accident and Emergency had not yet caught on) and the orthopaedic theatre, where Mr Lawrence Plewes, a Canadian orthopaedic surgeon, proved an excellent teacher. Major trauma often meant spilt brains and splintered bones and a month of them cured me of orthopaedic notions. It also made me a more careful driver.

The case that sticks in my memory was not a road accident, but a triple murder. One morning an ambulance brought in the bodies of a young mother and two children in their pyjamas. The husband worked for a chemical manufacturer and had run up huge debts which he could not handle and did not divulge to his wife. On the fatal day the family had returned from a holiday, which was presumably his farewell treat. That evening he poisoned them and himself with one of his company's products. There was undoubtedly more to the story than that, but the crime seemed cruel beyond belief.

I attended the post-mortem examinations which were performed by a Home Office pathologist and was present when the murderer regained consciousness, chained to the bed with a policeman by his side. The look on his face when he realised that he had killed his wife and children – but not himself – haunted me for weeks. It revived all my questions about a life hereafter and particularly about the children who were young and innocent. But nobody I spoke to at the hospital had answers.

For the second part of my elective, I went to an RAF hospital at Akrotiri in Cyprus. I wanted a closer look at what to expect when I was called up. In retrospect it was not a fair choice. Akrotiri was a kind of Shangri-La, a remote and beautiful place where life approaches perfection. It was far from typical as a posting.

The hospital stood on a promontory three miles from the flying station, with panoramic views over the Mediterranean.

Duties were not onerous, and the few patients were exceedingly well cared for. But whenever there was a terrorist attack or a hostage crisis in the Middle East, the hospital sprang into action and justified itself.

To my son Rob, who was then five years old, I wrote, 'I am staying on an island in the middle of the sea which is very hot and dry and beautiful. Every day I put on what you call my bus conductor's suit (i.e., tropical uniform), which is nice and cool. Everybody here wears bus conductor suits, except when they are on the beach when they wear almost nothing at all.'

The hospital worked tropical hours. The staff started very early in the morning and completed the doctoring by noon. Then everyone headed for the beaches.

The day before I arrived, a tragedy occurred. Part of the main beach was allocated to waterskiing and that area was marked by buoys and warning notices. But the lifeguards did not see a scuba diver who unwittingly swam into it. He surfaced in the path of a speeding boat and its keel cleaved his skull in two. He was the commanding officer of a fighter squadron stationed at Akrotiri and the speedboat was driven by one of his pilots.

Through this tragedy I met Squadron Leader Neil Flanagan, who performed the post-mortem examination. Neil was a haematologist who had a great love of pathology. He took me on trips into the interior of the island and showed me its medical facilities. In Limassol there was a large Greek hospital which was well equipped. In Famagusta, the Turkish hospital was a single storey building in a back street, no more than a cottage hospital. It was run by a Turkish Cypriot whom I shall call Dr Salma. His wife combined the roles of head nurse, pharmacist and manager.

Neil was good to Salma. He visited his hospital regularly, discussed patients with him and took away blood and urine samples for testing in the RAF lab. I recall one patient, a lady in her nineties from a mountain village. She never complained when a basal cell carcinoma developed on her cheek. Its other name is rodent ulcer, because it gnaws like a rat and devours surrounding tissues and bone. By the time her relatives brought her for medical attention, her face was like an anatomical dissection and nothing could be done. I did not have to go to Africa to see third world medicine after all.

Dr Salma struggled to keep his hospital going. Years later Neil told me about his downfall. A wealthy Turkish Cypriot had all the symptoms of a stomach ulcer and Salma offered to remove it surgically. In the hospital's tiny theatre he was surgeon-cum-anaesthetist, and his wife was his assistant, so there were no witnesses. He made a lengthy incision but was careful to cut through the skin and no deeper. Then he probably had a cup of coffee and read the newspaper. Then he sewed up.

Of course, you are thinking that this chicanery would have done no good at all. But medicine can play strange tricks. In this case it relieved the man of his symptoms as well as a pile of drachmas, at least for a while. Salma performed other pseudo-gastrectomies and the hospital prospered. Then one of the patients visited Turkey on holiday and there his ulcer perforated. He was rushed to a proper hospital where surgeons discovered the truth. The Salmas vanished and the hospital collapsed.

When I returned from Cyprus, the MBBS final examinations loomed. Nowadays medical students undergo periodic assessments which count towards the result, and any final examination may be something of an anticlimax, or so I am told. But in those days, finals were Judgment Day, Mount Everest and the London Marathon rolled into one.

As part of the preparation we attended 'grinds', which were so named because they were the most concentrated teaching of the entire course, and they could grind your confidence to powder. They were cramming sessions conducted by the hospital registrars and were held in a gloomy hall off Cleveland Street. The registrars, who were roughly my own age, were paid a small fee to try to get us through. One of them, Steve Haines (who appears in the next chapter), bombarded us with trick questions. If we answered incorrectly, he would say with a sneer, 'How much did you say this exam cost to take?'

And so eventually we came to the written examinations. I can only remember the obstetrics paper, which included the reasons for performing a Caesarean section. That was a godsend because Rob and Kate had both been Caesarean babies, and as a nervous dad I had interrogated the obstetricians closely on their management. I got good marks on that paper.

The practical part of finals was the 'clinicals,' when you were put in a room with a patient to take a history, make your examination and draw your conclusions. The examiner then grilled you on your findings.

Short clinicals were five minutes long; you were expected to diagnose the case without a full physical examination. We used to practise our skills from a distance on the London Underground. I once travelled with a friend and across the aisle was a lady with bulging eyes, perspiration and a twitch.

'Psst! See that? Overactive thyroid. Classic case.'

'Nah. She thinks you're ogling her.'

My first short case was nearly a disaster. He was a young man of healthy complexion dressed in T-shirt and jeans; he sat comfortably on a chair in the cubicle. On inquiry he had no symptoms and no complaints. Indeed, he seemed healthier than me. I wracked my brains but had no answer.

The minutes ticked by, and I was in a sweat. Then a bell rang and the examiner said, 'Thank you Mr Barton.' The young man stood up, grinned and slipped out. My eyes popped. He was barely four feet tall, a point that had escaped me in my nervousness. Confidence flooded back. 'Now, what's the answer, Mr Adam?'

'Ateliotic dwarfism, sir. Lack of anterior pituitary gland hormones.'

'Very good. Proceed to your long case.'

My eyes popped at what I had missed

In a long clinical case, the patient lay on a couch and you had half an hour to take a history and make a full physical examination. The patients were veterans whose condition altered little over time. This was their way of saying thank you to the NHS; all they got out of it was a day out, a small fee and numerous cups of tea. They were under instruction not to give the candidates too much help and never to reveal their diagnosis.

A Cockney gentleman lay on the couch displaying a belly so scarred that it looked like a snakes and ladder board. I asked him what I thought were the right questions and prodded, pressed and palpated his trunk and private parts. I finished up no wiser. Once again, I was stumped.

'Let's give you a hand on this one, doc,' he whispered, handing me a scrap of paper. 'Don't want yer to fail, do we?' On it were written a list of diagnoses, surgical operations and medications.

He gave me a wink. 'And while yer at it, 'ave a look at me old fife and drum. Got a few Nobby Stiles up there.'

Dr William Osler was an American physician who is regarded as one of the fathers of modern medicine. He taught students that a doctor who paid careful attention to his patients always learned from them. 'Listen to your patient,' he would say, 'he is telling you the diagnosis.' My long case was a prime example, though perhaps not quite what Osler had in mind.

Incidentally, the hint was to examine the gentleman's backside for haemorrhoids. 'Fife and drum' is Cockney rhyming slang for bum. Nobby Stiles was a popular English footballer and his name was slang for piles. (I have no idea if he suffered from them.)

About this time a friend called John Yeandle-Hignell was also striving to qualify. Like me he was an older man and making heavy weather of things. He decided to sit Conjoint, a qualification which was often used as a practice run before university finals. It was considered a softer option than MBBS and was probably too soft. It fell into disrepute and is no longer awarded.

At the end of a disastrous viva the examiner spoke in a kindly tone. 'Mr Yeandle-Hignell, I believe that you were formerly a seafaring man.'

'That is correct sir.'

'So do you have navigation experience?'

'Yes, I have my navigator's certificate.'

The examiner took him gently to a window. 'What do you see on those trees?'

'Um... leaves, sir.'

'Indeed. I suggest you navigate your passage out of here. When the trees are bare, you may navigate your way back. Good morning.'

Richard Gordon tells the same story in *Doctor in the House*. I suspect John's examiner adopted it for his personal use.

The elation at passing MBBS was enormous: a mixture of relief, gratitude and pride. Orchestras thundered, fireworks exploded, and bluebirds swarmed round my head. I was a doctor at last! I had completed the course on time and without a penny of debt.

Jacqui's friend Barbara Johnson sent a telegram of congratulations: 'Just because you're a doctor doesn't mean you can ask any girl to take off her clothes.'

The long student years during which my twenties slipped away, and my non-medical friends forged careers and fortunes were not easy. To be honest, I often pined for Fleet Street and the days of wine and roses. They had turned into laborious nights spent with books, bones and nappies. But in the end it was all worth it and I had many reasons to be grateful, especially to Jacqui and to our families.

And of course to the Middlesex, an excellent medical school, and to the many friends I made there. Together we absorbed the famous principle: 'To cure sometimes, relieve often and comfort always.' We also dissected, delivered, aspirated, palpated, sponged, bandaged, clerked and cannulated. Between the spikes of excitement, there were long plateaus of tedium. We spent countless hours pouring down microscopes and grilling each other on what was likely to 'come up' in the exams. We shared each other's triumphs and failures. We were in it together.

Some were more in it than others, for a close environment produces romance. Many of my contemporaries married nurses, radiographers, physiotherapists or other medical students. I was one of a minority who married off the reservation, so to speak. The majority of student marriages proved more enduring than those of the population at large. Long before we qualified and went our ways, we had forged life-long friendships.

Sadly there were those for whom medicine proved too great a challenge. The sensible ones knew it and changed to something else. Others soldiered on. The hospital paid lip service to the well-being of students and junior doctors, but some struggled and sank without the right support.

One was a quiet young man in my year called Colin, a thinker and a musician who took his life six months before MBBS finals. I remember him at a grand round a few weeks earlier. Grand rounds were held in a lecture hall, not on a ward, and were attended by senior and junior medical staff as well as students. There was much banter and professional one-upmanship, and we were often overawed. But not Colin: the lad presented a complex medical case to the professors and did it extremely well. Yet in his wastepaper basket the police found a sheet of paper with headings like 'clinical acumen,' 'bedside manner,' 'confidence,' 'musical achievements' and 'sex'. Against each he had placed a score out of ten. He judged himself too harshly by far.

It troubles me that there is no requirement for students to undergo a psychological assessment when they apply to read medicine, or for newly qualified doctors when they start their first job. This point will come up again when I consider Dr Harold Shipman, whose screwed-up character caused a tragedy of colossal proportions.

The Swinging Sixties are ancient history today and youngsters sometimes ask me, 'What was London like then? Was it awesome! Did you have a great time? Did you smoke pot?' My answer is, 'Sorry to disappoint you. Medical students had to be single minded. I had no time to swing. I was a husband and a father.'

Truth to tell, I had no desire to join the swinging scene. In my opinion the 1960s were not a brave new world. They were an insurrection against authority, order and right thinking. Time and again London was shaken by riots and sit-ins for causes that were harmful or socially irrelevant. City traders and hippies got high on hash while Mods and Rockers got high on amphetamines and fought each other and the police in the streets. The Beatles and a renegade American mathematician urged the world to try LSD. The music world was a cacophony of drugs, booze and free love.

Happily, the Middlesex insulated most of its fledglings from this insanity.

Did I do drugs? Yes. I took a couple of amphetamine pills on the eve of an examination. They kept me awake all night long, during which time I somehow correctly predicted half the questions in the paper. Two hours after finishing it, I could not remember a word I had written. I passed but I never repeated the experiment. As Scott Fitzgerald wrote: 'First you take a drink, then the drink takes a drink, then the drink takes you.'

9

Licensed to Kill

Newly qualified doctors were called housemen. They were 'on the house,' confined to the hospital for their first year and not legally permitted to practise outside it. Nowadays they are called F1s and F2s, names which have nothing to do with motor racing.

I set my heart on getting my first job at the Middlesex. I believed that the element of prestige would pay dividends. I also did not want to move my family from our comfortable basement flat in Victoria. I might not see much of them for six months, but they would be close at hand when I got away from my duties. I was wrong on both counts.

The affable John Ferguson (of the syphilitic finger) was my first choice of boss, but he took someone else, and I had to pay court to a less kindly character. This was Mr Cecil Murray who was nicknamed Slim. He dressed immaculately in a double-breasted grey suit with a matching silk tie and handkerchief. His interviews were informal; he sat in his theatre scrubs in the surgeons' changing room between operations, a cigarette dangling from his lips. He read my letter of application.

'Hmph, you are married, Adam. Don't care for married housemen. Children?'

'Two, sir.'

'Hmph. What'll you do with 'em?'

The outgoing houseman had warned me that only one answer was acceptable. Jacqui had agreed to it with mixed feelings.

'My wife will move out of London, to be nearer to her mother. Her father died a few months ago.'

'Hmph. Where?'

'Just outside Cheltenham, sir.'

Mr Murray's frown relaxed; it was far enough. He demanded total commitment from his junior staff. His patients rarely developed complications and he intended to keep it that way. He had been appointed a consultant in 1946 when being a general surgeon meant what it said. He would tackle anything from hernias to haemorrhoids and from gullets to gonads.

On a personal level he never seemed to appreciate my efforts or my sense of humour, and he communicated mainly in grunts. The one thing about which he was passionate was flyfishing. He once admitted that his life's ambition was to catch a 40-pound salmon.

On my first morning Steve Haines, the senior registrar, took me aside. 'Let's get one thing straight Andy. The job is not intended to be cushy. It's an endurance test. It sorts the successes out from the failures. I'll soon know which you are. Don't expect a social life. And don't expect sympathy – we've all been through it.'

Steve made a point of never helping a struggling houseman. 'You only learn by your mistakes' was his mantra. He never carried a stethoscope, which he disdainfully called guessing tubes, and he would request the loan of mine with a snap of the fingers.

As to the job, they called it 'treading the wards' and you walked miles every day, especially if your patients were spread around the hospital. But a better description was serving jail time. There was no protection from the European Union and no legal curb on your hours. You started at 6.00 a.m. and finished ten or twelve hours later. Some juniors claimed to be doing 120 hours a week, which worked out at 12 pence an hour. If you lived in the hospital, the administrators charged you for board and lodging.

Most of the work was clerical: clerking in new patients, re-examining old ones, ordering x-rays and lab tests, witnessing consent forms, and writing up drugs and discharge letters. Everything took for ever because it was done by hand. And things got lost so easily! X-ray films fell behind radiators, notes were misfiled, and lab reports vanished into thin air. You dashed between departments like a labrador retriever on the hunt. Computers, bar codes and pre-printed labels have made the work immeasurably easier.

Then there were the wretched pagers. All doctors except the consultants had to carry one. They only worked one-way, summoning you to a telephone with a shriek like a banshee (the banshee being a Gaelic spirit whose wailing warns of a death in the house, so the comparison is apt). You came to hate the darned thing; it was the enemy of your soul. On his last day of service one houseman got his revenge with a Black and Decker saw. He returned it in two pieces.

A sweet revenge

Your pager ensured that you had barely enough time to eat and no time for studying or relaxing with music or television. Sleep deprivation created mood changes and it was easy to make mistakes. A word of criticism felt like the end of the world.

I remember coming on duty in that mood and a staff nurse handing me a list of tasks that ran like something like this: 'Mr Bow pulled his catheter out and flooded the bed. Mr Griffith's drip has gone subcutaneous. The students can't get blood out of Mrs Banks. And you forgot to write your discharge summaries. Mr Simpson got fed up waiting and has called a taxi. He expects you to pay.'

The worst part was: 'Mrs Bailey's enema hasn't worked. Sister says please see to it.' That was the dreaded house officer's operation: the digital removal of impacted stools from a constipated patient.

My chum Paul Haycock had a worse time than me. He had a house physician's job on the Middlesex's cancer wing. It was a place which other doctors and students shunned. 'It was a six-month nightmare,' he recalled. 'I was treated like a serf. No students were placed there, so I had to take all the bloods and perform all the chores. The consultants barely spoke to me and gave me no teaching. The registrar refused me practical help, even when a patient bled torrentially after an operation. The worst thing was being ordered, from time to time and with no discussion, to give a liberal dose of morphine to a dying patient. The only skill I acquired was aspirating pleural effusions.' That was using a syringe to suck out fluid created by malignant deposits around the lungs.

The hospital had no accommodation for married doctors, and Paul was married. He lived in a single room containing an iron bedstead, a telephone and a table. He had two days off in six months and came to loath the place.

His next job was as a house surgeon in Vancouver in Canada. 'When I got there, I was welcomed with opened arms and found myself surrounded by a wonderful team of nurses, phlebotomists and paramedics. The hospital food was amazing, and the administration had reserved married accommodation for us on site. At lunchtime I went into the hospital bank to enquire about the possibility of a loan and by teatime I owned a Ford Mustang.' In time Paul returned to the UK, but not surprisingly he never worked in the NHS.

We were expected to acquire some surgical experience but the registrars (who were also in training posts) took whatever the chief left, and left the crumbs. We performed bedside procedures which nurses do today and do far better. Non-teaching hospitals were different; a house surgeon who showed promise might open abscesses, remove cysts, and extirpate in-growing toenails. He might even perform an appendicectomy under supervision.

A friend of mine went from being house surgeon at the Middlesex to senior house officer in a south-coast town. Months later he told me the story in the King and Queen. On his first day a secretary handed him a piece of paper. The conversation went as follows.

'What's this?'

'Mr Fogarty's circumcisions list.'

'Who does them?'

'You do. At 2.00 p.m. in clinic.'

My friend drew on his pint and sighed. 'Tricky, eh? I couldn't admit ignorance. I spent lunch time reading *Pye's Surgical Handicraft*. Then I did the snip on four kids. I thought everything went well. At the time.'

He used the traditional cutting method rather than applying a clamp which makes the foreskin wither and fall off after a few days. That evening three pale small boys were admitted with various degrees of blood loss. My chum had omitted to place stitches on branches of the dorsal artery of the penis.

He sighed. 'Of course, the one who really worried me was the little fellow who did not come back. I often wondered what happened to him.'

Consultants' private patients were a source of grievance. The Labour minister, Aneurin Bevan, boasted that he introduced the NHS in 1948 'by stuffing the doctors' mouths with gold.' By this he meant that consultants who agreed to work part-time in the NHS were allowed to continue seeing private patients and to treat them in private facilities.

Most consultants in London earned fat sums this way, expecting their housemen to look after the patients with the same diligence as their NHS ones. If you wanted the job you had to grin and bear it. You helped your chief build his fortune, but you rarely if ever received any reward. (When a registrar helped out in theatre, he always got some.)

The injustice of the situation inspired a fine story around the time of the Apollo 11 moon launch in 1969. It claimed that before the launch, the NASA bosses faced a crisis. The lawyers insisted that an orthopaedic surgeon accompany the astronauts to the moon. But every surgeon whom they contacted wanted millions of dollars and the budget was overdrawn. Finally, they rang up a Harley Street consultant. After a short pause, he said he would be happy to oblige.

'How much would you charge, Sir Henry?'

'An appropriate remuneration is 5,000 guineas, in advance.' (A guinea was then equivalent to a pound and a shilling, or five new pence. Britain had ceased to mint them, but doctors and lawyers found them a handy way to boost their income.)

'Guineas? Why guineas?'

'My fee is £5,000. The shillings are for my registrar who will be making the trip.' As a houseman working for a miserly chief, I loved that joke.

On Saturday mornings, after spending all week with NHS patients, I assisted Mr Murray in theatre with his private patients. Even on my weekends off. I was responsible for the administrative and clerical details, but in theatre I did little more than wield a retractor or a suction tube. I was occasionally permitted to stitch a wound if it was a small one.

On a typical weekend I caught a train after lunch from Paddington to Evesham, where Jacqui was waiting in our ancient Morris Minor. We reached our rented home outside Cheltenham by mid-afternoon, for a rapturous reunion with Rob and Kate. As the hours passed, I was conscious that I had to be back on the wards the next day, to clerk in a new batch of patients. I had less than 24 hours with my family every fortnight. Convicts on compassionate leave get a better deal.

Jacqui felt the loneliness of her situation, but in truth she complained very little. She was grieving her father's death and supporting her mother as best she could. She cared for our two children single-handedly through minor illness and accidents, which also included the death of our family dog.

I conclude this passage of pathos by recalling that most consultants were wholly unsympathetic to the grievances of their juniors. They had all come through the system which, as Steve Haines said, sifted the successes from the failures, and they had emerged as thundering successes. Naturally they approved the system. They even opposed a request to pay us overtime payments because, as one consultant told *The Middlesex Hospital Journal,* 'That would lower the standing of the profession to that of a car mechanic.'

When the British Medical Association was eventually persuaded to press for overtime payments, it proposed a threshold of 100 hours a week. With friends like that, we wondered, who needed enemies?

* * *

Nevertheless, there was a lot of fun in being a house surgeon at the Middlesex Hospital and a lot of experience to pick up if you hung around and used your eyes. The chief place for doing that was the Casualty Department. On 'take' nights we had to examine any patient whom a casualty officer thought required admission. Patients were still known as casualties, a term which lumped together the dead, the wounded and the sick.

Many of them came from Soho, which was in our backyard. It was a veritable Babylon with its night clubs, strip joints, sex cinemas and gay bars. Every weekend we dealt with drunks, prostitutes, drug addicts and meth drinkers, as well as the poor wraiths who hung around the department for no clear reason. It was said that no one who lived in Soho drew a pension because they all died young.

I learned a lot from the casualty porter, David Evans, who was appointed in 1934. 'You young gents have it easy,' he would say. 'You should have seen Soho before it was cleaned up. It was a den of everything nasty. Friday night was Skull Night. The roughs would draw their pay, drink half of it and start beating people up. We might get two or three fractured skulls in an evening.'

In 1959 the government passed the Street Offences Act which cleared the prostitutes from Soho's streets. They went off to Paddington and the troublemakers followed them. 'Good riddance,' said David, 'St Mary's had to sort 'em out.'

He warned us about the scroungers who were after a free bed for a night. They would pin a safety pin inside their vest and when a chest x-ray was taken it would scare the doctor into admitting them. One chap had a large dent in his skull, the result of an accident he'd suffered years earlier. He would grip his head in his hands, moan piteously and pretend that he had been knocked down by a car.

I was invited by a casualty officer to examine an elderly man who had undergone a tracheotomy for cancer of the throat. 'It's an occasional complication,' he said, 'Have a look and tell me what you think.'

The poor man sat bolt upright on the side of the cot, wheezing through a hole at the root of his neck. The opening was distorted and the skin red. It looked very painful.

'He's developed an abscess alongside the trachea,' I said confidently. 'I suspect bacterial contamination on the endotracheal tube. If I press here ...'

'Don't!' cried the casualty officer, backing away. He was too late. Most abscesses have gooey contents like melted Camembert, but this one was fresh and liquid. At my touch it ruptured and discharged into the man's airway. He gave a gargantuan cough and emitted a fountain of brown-green fluid from his neck. It showered both of us, like Vesuvius erupting.

The casualty doctor glowered. 'You idiot! You never do that without putting on a mask. Always treat an abscess like a nun, with respect.'

The patient coughed a few times to clear the gunk and shook himself like a spaniel. 'Blimey, thanks doc!' he said to me. 'That's done the trick. I feel better now.'

* * *

The patients you saw in the Casualty Department were soon forgotten during a busy week. The ward patients were the ones whom you got to know, and you learned more from them than how to practise medicine. They taught you about courage and perseverance. My favourite definition of the word patient is one who bears suffering without complaint. And patients are the only people in a hospital who are entirely sane, because they want to escape from it as soon as possible. The staff choose to spend their lives surrounded by sickness and suffering.

One delightful patient whom I shall call Mr Good was seen by Mr Murray in Harley Street and admitted the same day. He was a gentleman in his forties with an attractive fiancée. When clerking him in, I asked what his employment was.

'I'm a professional gambler.'

'Wow, I've never met one before. May I ask what you bet on?'

'I play the horses and please don't ask for a tip, doctor. I bet two or three times a year and I spend a fortune getting the right information. Otherwise it's a mug's game. Lady Luck is a fickle wench.'

Actually, Lady Luck had already smiled upon Mr Good that week, and on his rectum to be precise. When Mr Murray examined him for anal bleeding, the extreme tip of his index finger detected a cancer located high up in the rectum. That was a classic example of the surgical maxim, 'If you don't put your finger in it, you'll put your foot in it.'

Murray took great pains in excising the cancer and his dissection saved Mr Good a colostomy bag. I looked after his post-operative care, and he went home relieved and grateful.

There was a sequel to the tale. A few weeks later my mother came up to town. She took one look at me and exclaimed, 'Darling, how thin you are! Aren't you eating properly?'

I did not like to tell her that most housemen lost a stone and that my dinner was often baked beans in my bedroom at midnight. Instead, I made light of the matter and took her to dinner at a chic Italian restaurant as if that were my usual practice. I had not eaten there before, and quickly realized that it was far beyond my budget.

Halfway through the meal I spotted Mr Good and his lady at another table and waved. He came over, pumped my hand, and made some very complimentary remarks. Mother was thrilled. 'What a nice man!'

An hour later I called for the bill and nearly had a fit at the total. As I prepared to empty my wallet (this happened long before credit cards) the waiter said, 'All taken care of, sir. The gentleman on table six paid your bill before he left.' I was extremely grateful for Mr Good's old-world courtesy. My mother almost swooned with maternal pride.

Many of our cases were technically demanding. The Middlesex was renowned for taking difficult cases referred from other hospitals and Mr Murray's genius lay in the surgery of the stomach and duodenum. Partial gastrectomy was still the standard treatment for peptic ulcers, and we had plenty of those. His *tour de force* was the Whipple's procedure. Known technically as a pancreatico-duodenectomy, it is an operation performed for cancer of the pancreas and takes between four and twelve hours depending on the approach used. It is the ultimate test of a surgeon's skill and endurance.

One patient who underwent this operation was a successful inventor who was a millionaire and an alcoholic. He was clearly nervous, and questioned me on every detail. The anaesthetist was Dr Brian Sellick, a senior consultant who gassed at Mr Murray's private ops. On this occasion he too was nervous. He gave me a call.

'Adam, if your boss takes as long on this chap as he did on his last Whipple's, we'll all be in trouble.'

'Why's that, sir?'

'I've just seen his liver function tests. If he's off alcohol for long, he'll get delirium tremens and cease to be a stationary target. Make sure you take the necessary steps, my boy.'

He rang off before I could ask what he meant by necessary steps. I had to ask the ward sister. She was a no-nonsense lady.

'Don't they teach you that at medical school? What you need is a funnel, a plastic pipe, some KY jelly and some alcohol. It's like a gastric wash-out in reverse.'

'You mean ...'

'Yes, an alcohol enema. Get your patient on his side and don't give him too much in one go. The rectum absorbs fluids rapidly and they can get pissed without a hint of alcohol on their breath.'

In those days alcohol was prescribed as an appetite stimulant and every ward had some in the drugs cupboard. My patient's tipple was cognac but given the unusual mode of administration I figured that he would not tell it from cooking brandy. I gave him the cheap stuff and he was quite happy.

I had other memorable patients, one of them Sir Douglas Ranger, the next dean of the medical school and a perfect gentleman. After a tricky operation he rewarded me with a fine set of cut-glass tumblers and some excellent whisky to put in them. At the other end of the social spectrum was Fred D., a roguish old Cockney with widespread cancer. Sister Chris Cubitt managed him beautifully until he was discharged to die in a care home. Before leaving he gave me a box of chocolates. 'Here y'are doc, I won't be needing these now.' I later learned he had been one of Scotland Yard's most wanted men. He served more than thirty years in prison.

Another patient had two wives, each of whom was ignorant of the other's existence. He begged the nurses to help him keep it that way. They did a brilliant job controlling the visiting hours of the ladies, wafting them in and out like actors in a Whitehall Theatre farce so they did not meet. I wondered at the time if that made us all accomplices to bigamy.

* * *

Christmas 1969 came at last. Nobody wants to spend Christmas in hospital, but at the Middlesex we managed to give it colour and fun. The previous year, two of my student firm padded themselves out with cushions. Garvin Falkus was hoisted onto the shoulders of Peter Barnes so that, clothed in an outsized white coat, they became a Goliath nine feet tall. While the ward sister was absent, they conducted a spoof ward round of their own. The patients were so awestruck at the towering figure that none could answer even simple questions about the state of their bowels.

Christmas started with a concert revue that was even funnier and more irreverent than usual. As Christmas Day approached, we discharged as many patients as possible and merged two wards into one. The nurses decorated the rooms with trees and holly, and bought chocolates and soap for the patients. On Christmas Eve they toured the wards singing carols by torchlight, their cloaks turned inside out to display the scarlet linings. I am sure Charles Dickens would have approved.

Next morning the consultants donned paper hats and carved several turkeys with much jollity. The housemen dressed up as Santa or wore elf ears; they shook hands in a manly way and wished each other the season's greetings. The student nurses pinned mistletoe in their hair and allowed themselves to be kissed in the sluice by the students.

On his way out Mr Murray said farewell and handed me an envelope. I felt a warm flush of success. Recognition at last! Later I opened it. It contained a book token of small denomination tucked inside a gift card. The donor's name was partly erased, and it was not Mr Murray's. The gift was second hand.

Six months as a house surgeon served their purpose. I survived the endurance test and realized that a surgeon's life was not for me. In an emergency I could apply a tourniquet and perhaps perform a tracheotomy, but the responsibility and the fear of mistakes were too high for my disposition. Much of the time I felt a sense of foreboding, even when things were going well. It was as if a wheel were about to come off the cart and land me in a ditch.

Happily there were no disasters. Cecil Murray was a perfectionist, and dying under his care was not allowed. I did not write one death certificate. That would change during the next six months.

* * *

That Christmas is my last memory of a place which was highly formative in my life, and where our daughter Kate was born. It seemed indestructible at the time, like one of London's historic monuments. But nobody foresaw the extent of the NHS reforms in the next decade which reduced London's teaching hospitals from twelve to five. At one point the Middlesex was offered a lifeline, a green field site in the suburbs. It declined the offer and staff members with no interest in private practice held the consultants responsible. 'Greedy beggars! Too attached to Harley Street, four minutes away by taxi.'

If that were true, their self-interest cost them dear. In 1974 the hospital lost its autonomy, and in order to survive it had to function in partnership with University College Hospital, which was a far larger concern. So did the medical school. Soon both were forced to merge with it.

A marriage of equals was envisaged but amalgamation tuned into annihilation. The name Middlesex vanished, and the hospital was levelled to the ground. A mass of apartments, offices and shops sprang up in their place. The chapel alone survived, thanks to its Grade II listing. It is the only reminder of countless nurses and doctors who cared for the sick and the needy for 270 years. The names of nurses who perished in epidemics while caring for their patients are inscribed on its walls.

The new owners spent a great deal of money restoring the chapel, which the *Daily Telegraph* called 'the most beautiful room in London you probably didn't know about.' It had never been consecrated so they were able to shape it their way. It is now known as the Fitzrovia Chapel and among other things is an events venue. Today the ghosts of the past look down on art exhibitions and fashion shows.

10

Salisbury General Infirmary

In my first week at the Salisbury General Infirmary a surgeon leaned across the dining room table and asked with a grin, 'Have you met the grey lady? You will soon! She lives in the attic over your wards. She always appears when a patient dies. You lot keep her busy.'

In that era grey ladies were common in old hospitals. They were the ghosts of nurses who had been spurned by a lover or were tormented by the memory of a nursing disaster. The ambience of the Salisbury General Infirmary encouraged you to believe in them. Florence Nightingale had advised on its design and the wings were long Nightingale-style wards with creaking wooden floors, heavy arched doors, and shadowy corners. They held thirty or more patients. You could imagine the Lady with the Lamp moving quietly from bed to bed, closing the eyelids of the dying.

The grey lady at work

On our first morning the senior house officer (SHO) in medicine, a bright young physician called Andrew Marshall, gave the new housemen a pep talk. He told us rural Wiltshire was not like London's West End. 'The locals are no weaklings – they don't seek attention until late in the day. And when they do, they expect the GP to treat them at home. They're on their last legs if they reach us. You'll see anaemias so severe they can't walk, and end-stage cancers that have never been investigated.'

Did he exaggerate? Not at all. Most gastric haemorrhages at Salisbury seemed to be torrential and most infections life-threatening. Even the dermatologist joked that he saw cases of acne in a terminal stage. Why was this? You have to realize that doctor-patient relationships in 1970 were different from today. Patients had limited expectations of what could be done for them; they trusted their doctors and nurses implicitly and were pathetically grateful for their help. Things began to change in the 1990s with the introduction of the Patients' Charter, health pressure groups, the internet and other mixed blessings.

As a house physician it was depressing to admit so many stoical, bewildered folk who struggled to keep going until their last hour. You barely had time to obtain a history and order lab tests before they breathed their last. You needed to reach a diagnosis as quickly as possible, for without one you couldn't write a death certificate. The family then had the additional stress of a coroner's post-mortem examination.

* * *

Despite these pressures, I took immediately to the infirmary. It stood in the centre of the pleasant bustling city, close to the cathedral and the water meadows immortalized by John Constable. The clear waters of the Hampshire Avon flowed alongside it.

It had a homely atmosphere. Hospitals today are run by vast teams of managers and administrators who are obsessed with targets and protecting their jobs. In Salisbury, the infirmary was run by an excellent secretary-manager called Miss Dorothy Macey who worked hand in hand with the Matron. Everyone from the cleaners and porters to the consultants was exceedingly friendly and greeted you with a cheerful 'Good morning!' or 'Hello doctor!'

The on-call doctors lived in the Poplars, a Georgian mansion in the hospital grounds where a wonderful lady called Gladys Elliott cleaned the rooms, prepared evening meals, and spoiled us like children. In spare moments (of which there were not many) we relaxed in the garden and spun Frisbees back and forth; the craze had just arrived from America. There was a hospital tennis court too.

The less convenient part was that when the cardiac bleep sounded, the duty house physician had to dash 100 yards from the Poplars to the hospital, climb two flights of stairs and somehow find enough breath to perform cardio-pulmonary resuscitation.

The Middlesex Hospital and Salisbury General Infirmary had several things in common. Both dated from the 18th century and were associated with famous names. Both were bursting at the seams and had nowhere to expand. They suffered similar fates. The Middlesex was bulldozed, while the infirmary was replaced by a brand-new district hospital outside the city in the 1990s.

The site was gobbled up by developers who turned the main building into luxury apartments. If the grey lady still haunts the corridors, she must wonder where the beds went.

* * *

The infirmary had three consultant physicians, a registrar, an SHO and three house physicians. The latter worked three days on call for emergency admissions and four days off, then vice versa. It made a social life difficult to plan, but at least I had one. I went home to my family and slept in my own bed, which was a welcome change.

We struggled with a lack of facilities. We had no ultrasound equipment and only a limited number of cardiac monitors. There was an intensive therapy unit (ITU) but no coronary care unit. Once I rode with a desperately ill patient in an ambulance to the cardio-thoracic centre in Southampton, a 25-mile journey with lights flashing and siren blaring.

The Casualty Department was pretty basic too. It was run by the two surgical SHOs who were often expected to be in two places at once. They were assisted by a GP during the day and overseen by orthopaedic surgeons in Oxford, which was seventy miles away. The physicians' domain included an old wartime hospital at Odstock (just south of the city), whose other occupant was the regional plastic surgery unit. One consultant, Dr Longridge, had a ward of stroke patients in a Nissen hut and I accompanied him there on his ward rounds.

There were no junior physicians at Odstock, and I asked what the arrangements were for cardiac arrests and other emergencies. The answer was: 'There's no problem because none of the patients are for resuscitation. If you're on call and there's an emergency elsewhere, drive quickly and don't worry about the police.'

I was told about a GP who was called to the home of a child in an asthma crisis. After he drove through a red light a police car overtook him and signalled him to stop. The GP waved his stethoscope out of the window and carried on regardless.

'Wow!' I said admiringly. 'Did he save the child?'

'Yes, happily. The policeman hung around and when the doctor emerged, he drove past him shaking his handcuffs out of the window. As a warning.'

It was a nice story, but over the years I heard it in other parts of the country, once during the funeral of an elderly paediatrician. It is probably an urban myth.

I cannot omit my appreciation of the nurses. Salisbury had a small nursing school which dated back to 1870. Florence Nightingale intervened in its affairs more than once to improve the nurses' pay and conditions, and she was a lasting inspiration to them.

The nurses were red-cheeked local girls who were bright, good hearted and excellent at their job. They took seriously the infirmary's motto: *The needy and the sick shall not always be forgotten.* They did not forget exhausted junior doctors either, and made toast and coffee to keep us going through the small hours.

That struck a bell with my father, who was a house physician at St. Thomas' Hospital in London, in the 1930s. He told me, 'The Nightingales were very good to us, but one doctor made a pest of himself. He used to raid the ward kitchens and help himself to their snacks. The midwives got fed up with it. One night he was offered a mug of hot chocolate.

'Yummy! Nice and creamy,' he said, smacking his lips as he guzzled it.

'It should be,' said a midwife. 'I made it especially for you, doctor. With milk expressed from Mrs Jenkins' breasts. She's overproducing and leaking into the sheets.'

* * *

The house physicians were often busy writing death certificates and, though I never saw her, the grey lady cannot have had much rest. Bodies for cremation required a cremation certificate as well. We had to examine them in the mortuary and if we found a cardiac pacemaker we removed it, to prevent the crematorium oven blowing up. The fee that was paid was known as the 'ash cash'.

By agreement we pooled the money and treated ourselves and our spouses or girl friends to a slap-up dinner each month. Most of the dinners took place at The Silver Plough at Pitton, which became Wiltshire's first gastronomic pub. These outings were a source of puzzlement to the other customers. At the conclusion of the meal, the president of the doctors' mess rose and proposed a toast: 'Ladies and gentlemen, to the Ashes!' Nobody could understand our enthusiasm for test cricket in a year when no Australian series was played.

Drug company reps also stood us dinners, in a thinly veiled attempt to influence our prescribing habits. One benefactor we called Mister Mogadon and another Mister

Mandrax, after the sedatives which their companies manufactured. They competed with each other to stage the finest meal in a nice restaurant, and we naughtily egged them on. Both drugs subsequently went out of favour, as did the practice of gastronomic bribery.

* * *

One night in February 1970 a 28-year-old woman was rushed to the hospital by ambulance. When I saw her in the Casualty Department she was hunched on a stretcher, a blanket round her shoulders, shaking uncontrollably. Her dilated pupils made her look like a frightened rabbit.

'It's a bad 'un, doctor,' said the ambulance driver. 'She's been hoarding her drugs.' I read rapidly through her notes. At the age of eighteen she had given birth to a baby which her family made her surrender for adoption. From then on, she was tormented by guilt. After her marriage (to a man who was not the father), she refused to have other children. The marriage deteriorated and so did her mental state. She was referred to the psychiatrists, but they could not help her. This was her second suicide attempt.

'Will I die this time, doctor?' she asked in a tiny voice. 'Please, let me die.' That was all she would say.

'No,' I replied as firmly as I could. 'We won't let that happen.' But I knew that I lied. The medical situation was desperate. She had taken a massive dose of antidepressant tablets and waited for four hours before calling an ambulance. What made things worse was that she had vomited nothing. She soon became unconscious. We performed a gastric lavage and spent the night administering fluids and diuretic drugs in an effort to drive the poison out of her system and keep her blood pressure and heart going.

After she had spent 28 hours in a coma, she started to move her limbs and to respond to pin prick stimuli. Then she lapsed into an abnormal heart rhythm which proved impossible to reverse. We struggled to resuscitate her for over an hour before giving up.

Dr Bob Pinkerton was the head of pathology at Salisbury General Infirmary. He performed the post-mortem examination on the girl and asked me to call on him after my day's work. His office was in keeping with his position. As I relaxed in a leather armchair, I admired the oak panelling and the cocktail cabinet concealed in a bookcase. Pathologists did not seem to do too badly, I noted.

'How about a well-deserved scotch, Dr Adam?' he said, opening the cabinet. 'I have a favour to ask. I edit the hospital journal and I want you to write up the overdose case for publication.' I could not easily refuse and while researching the subject of tri-cyclic antidepressants I discovered something surprising. By the time she died, our patient had passed a critical point. Her drug level had peaked, and it was actually declining. It made the tragedy seem even greater.

She was a year younger than me, and her death shook me. It was a vivid demonstration of the destructive power of grief. Few people apart from romantic novelists seemed to know much about it at the time. The chronic grief syndrome had only recently been named but I had heard of it and wrote a paper about it during my final year as a medical student. I took Queen Victoria as a case history; she was widowed with nine children at the age of 41. After the death of Prince Albert, she went into mourning for forty years and her withdrawal from society had political repercussions.

What had previously been theory was suddenly raw and real. The case demonstrated the psychological harm that is caused when the mother-child bond is broken, and a baby is aborted or given away. The Abortion Act had been passed three years earlier and there was little real understanding of the price that women pay. More than fifty years later, when there is no shortage of evidence, the pro-choice lobby minimizes it.

One of the duties of the on-call medical team in Salisbury was to refer overdose patients to a psychiatrist. She would advise them how to cope with their problems, to persuade them from attempting suicide again. Our faith in the system was shaken when the psychiatrist in question took an overdose herself and was admitted through Casualty. Hoping to avoid detection, she gave a false name but was quickly rumbled.

11

Near-Death Experiences

My most memorable patient at the Salisbury General Infirmary was a 72-year-old retired Indian army officer with the unforgettable name of Lieutenant-Colonel Humphrey St John Carruthers. He was commissioned in 1915 at the age of eighteen, fought in two world wars and commanded a battalion of the Ghurka Rifles. He was admitted to the infirmary three days after suffering severe chest pain. An electrocardiogram and blood tests confirmed a recent heart attack. Three days later he had another one.

The timing was spectacular because the ward was packed with visitors and his family were gathered round the bed. Probably the excitement of seeing them triggered the event. A crash call went out and we revived him with cardio-pulmonary resuscitation and a defibrillator behind a flimsy curtain. A pop-eyed audience sat on the other side of it. One visitor whispered, 'I watched *Emergency Ward 10* for years and it's rubbish compared with this.'

We moved the colonel to a side room where we 'specialled' ill patients when there was no room on the ITU. It had no special staff or equipment except for piped oxygen and the crash trolley in a corner, along with the buckets and mops.

We intubated him, put him on a ventilator and gave him sedation. Thirty minutes later he had another cardiac arrest and we shocked him back to life again. At this point Andrew Marshall summoned the housemen to a council of war. 'Look,' he said, 'The man's a living legend. We can't give up without a fight. There's no evidence of lasting damage to his heart so far. We may be able to save him, but it's going to take a combined effort. What do you think?'

We agreed and arranged our rotas so that one of us was always near the side room, ready to leap into action. That was the best we could do. Effective methods of treating heart attacks, like by-pass surgery and stents to keep blocked arteries open, were either not invented or not available outside a major centre. Patients were prescribed three weeks of bed rest and tranquillizers to keep them quiet. During that time they might fall victim to pulmonary emboli, bed sores or lethal boredom.

In a few years all that would change. The same patients would be rapidly mobilised and sent home, with far better results.

But this was 1970 and the colonel remained highly unstable. Over the course of the next few days his heart stopped, and he 'died' no less than 27 more times. On each occasion we shocked him and brought him back. All these efforts were made on top of our normal duties. There was one 36-hour stint during which I got three hours sleep.

It took four days to persuade the colonel's heart to settle down. His chest, after receiving so many shocks of electricity, resembled a seared steak, but his mental faculties were as sharp as ever. When he got home he wrote to the *Daily Telegraph* commending the hospital staff for their efficiency. To me he wrote, 'In some ways it has really been like spending a short period with a first-class regiment.'

That was without doubt the nicest compliment I received as a house physician, but the colonel made a lasting impression on me for a different reason. When he learned that I was an RAF officer, he treated me as a comrade-in-arms. He wanted to tell me what happened to him in the twilight zone that exists between life and death. It was so extraordinary that I asked him to write it down. I have kept his account all these years.

He related it to me in detail as he sat in the day room in his dressing gown, consulting his notes. He was making good progress and getting stronger by the day. He spoke like a soldier reporting a sortie into no man's land, in a clipped precise tone.

'I've never had religious convictions. And believe me Dr Adam, nothing remotely like this ever happened to me before!'

He remembered collapsing with pain after the second heart attack. Almost immediately he came out of his body and the pain ceased. He passed down a dark tunnel, through a gate, and into a brightly lit garden. There he met a person dressed in sandalwood-coloured robes; there was no doubt in his mind it was Jesus. There was no crown of thorns, no wounds on his hands or feet. 'The expression on his face was of indescribable beauty. His eyes particularly were full of understanding, forgiveness and a wonderful sympathy.' The colonel's own eyes filled with tears.

He was allowed to approach within inches. He felt an amazing elation and longed to remain close, but a voice told him that he had to go back. He returned reluctantly along the tunnel. The next thing he knew he was back in his bed and the pain had returned. There were other details, but that was the heart of the story.

With his permission I related it to my colleagues; none had heard of such a thing and they looked blank. 'It's a hallucination, Andy. Brought on by the stress of 29 cardiac arrests, no doubt. And look at the drugs we gave him.'

I was not convinced. The Latin word *hallucinari* means 'to wander or ramble in the mind.' Hallucinations are confused and frightening events that are devoid of meaning. Patients who get them are disorientated; they pull out their drips, fall out of bed and later do not remember what happened.

Nor was I convinced that drugs were the answer, or the whole answer. I had read Aldous Huxley's *Doors of Perception* and every pop star at the time seemed to be on magic mushrooms and having out-of-body experiences. But theirs were not detailed and coherent experiences like this one. Nor had we given the colonel a drug that was known to cause an out-of-body experience, and we kept him well ventilated and oxygenated.

Subconsciously I wanted to believe there was something significant beyond this life and that the colonel had discovered a key. At the first opportunity I scoured the hospital library but found nothing in the medical literature. The term 'near-death experience' had not yet been coined. That happened five years later, when an American psychiatrist named Dr Raymond Moody presented a study that described 150 contemporary cases.

Let me explain what was happening in the medical world at this time. The 1970s saw rapid advances in neurosurgery and in cardiac and accident surgery. Coronary care units and ITUs were springing up and surgeons and anaesthetists were taking patients to places they had never been before. They were coming back with stories like that of Colonel Carruthers and demanding an explanation. Doctors were forced to pay attention to their anxiety and to do something about it. (That's a healthy thing in medicine and does not happen often enough.) There was no point in referring them to the shrinks because the shrinks had no answers either.

Eventually clinicians began to take the subject seriously and publish single cases. Then they published series of cases in tens, then scores, then hundreds. Near-death experiences became accepted by many doctors as a genuine medical event. Today there are thousands of well-documented cases in medical journals and thousands more on websites. I have come across more than fifty paperbacks written by individuals who claim to have had the experience.

A working definition of a near-death experience runs something like this: 'a profound psychological and spiritual event which has mystical other worldly features and usually happens to individuals who are close to death or in a potentially life-threatening situation.'

Most subjects believe they go to heaven, or something like it, and have been in the presence of supernatural beings who are either angels or someone they call God or Jesus. Their experiences include coming out of their body, seeing and hearing what is going on at the scene where they 'died,' passing through a tunnel, encountering a beautiful light, and meeting friends and relatives who have died. They have a heightened awareness of everything around them, and say that they felt far more alive than before they died.

Many also acquire what philosophers have long regarded as the Holy Grail, an understanding of the universe. It covers things past, present and to come. It is probably what the bible means when it says, 'Now we see only a reflection as in a mirror; then we shall see face to face' (1 Corinthians 13:12).

With regard to their lives on earth, many individuals experience a panoramic review. Past events flash before their eyes which they see from the viewpoint of others as well as of themselves. A voice interprets why this or that thing happened, but without judgment or condemnation. Their life is interpreted to them in terms of value and not of achievements.

As Colonel Carruthers discovered, an intense feeling of love and acceptance permeates everything. Soldiers, prison officers and hardened businessmen break down in tears when they try to describe it. It is the reason that those who have these experiences long to return and to take as many people with them as they can.

Some people think that near-death experiences only occur in countries with a Christian culture. That is not so. Scientific papers from around the world show they are universal. They happen to individuals of any age, sex, race, religious belief and social background. Atheists, agnostics and 'bad people' have experiences like those of religious people.

When you consider their number, complexity and implications, your first question must be, 'Are they authentic or an illusion?' Two things convince me that they are authentic.

One is the high degree of agreement between the accounts in both their major and minor details. Fifteen to twenty core features have been described; some people experience a few and others experience many. No two experiences are the same, but they agree uncannily in the nature of the details.

The second argument is that of cause and effect. If a person claims to have gone to heaven, to have been in the presence of God, to have spoken with angels and to have had knowledge of the universe, you would expect him or her to be changed. I do not mean just in the here and now, but twenty or more years down the line.

That is what happens; there are decades of follow-up in the medical literature to prove it. Dr Moody said that in twenty years he did not find one person who had not undergone a significant spiritual and psychological change. Eighty per cent say, 'I was changed forever.' They define their lives as before and after their near-death experience.

Transformation is not too strong a word. People come back as different personalities. They experience inner healing and peace and for the first time have a caring and compassionate attitude towards others. This is particularly true of men. Their wives are no doubt astonished at the changes.

I sometimes wondered how long a reprieve we gave Colonel Carruthers. Did he see Christmas 1970? Was it worth the ordeal? While researching for this book I was delighted to find the answer on a website of British Indian Army officers. In fact, he lived nineteen more years, before dying at the age of 91 in North London. A remarkable achievement. He would have had many opportunities to dine off his experience.

* * *

Years after my time in Salisbury, I studied near-death experiences in depth and spoke about them when I was a guest speaker on board cruise ships. That talk always got a full house. The audience included people who had undergone an experience and never told anyone because they feared they would appear unhinged.

At the end of each talk I would make an invitation: Jacqui and I would be in a certain lounge that day and if anyone wanted to discuss their near-death experience, I would be happy to meet them. We were surprised at the number of people who came, and what we learned from them. Their relief at being able to revisit their experience over a cup of tea was immense, and I know we helped many to find a greater understanding and peace. I treasure a bundle of letters, written on ship's stationery.

I remember two ladies in the front row who followed my talk with rapt attention. I told how some people, after a near-death experience, undergo a change in their body's electromagnetic field. Their digital watches go haywire, and radios and microwave ovens malfunction in their presence. At this point, the younger woman dug the older one in the ribs and giggled. Later I asked them what was up.

'It's Mum,' the daughter explained. 'She had a near-death experience two years ago. Now whenever she goes into her living room, the television switches channels. And we had to buy her a wind-up watch. We thought she was a bit, you know, 'touched' by it all. Thanks for explaining!'

Scientists have turned near-death experiences into a battlefield. The traditionalists say they are scientifically impossible. If your brain is dead (which they claim is the situation in cardiac arrest) you are wholly dead and there is no possibility of cognitive activity like thinking, reasoning and remembering. Therefore near-death experiences must happen after the event, and be imaginary.

Traditionalists also maintain that for an event to be accepted as a fact, you must be able to reproduce it in a laboratory. But that argument begs the question, since you cannot reproduce a near-death experience without the risk of causing the real thing. No ethical committee would permit it.

Nor is everything that is true capable of being proved scientifically. For example, I am 180 cm tall and weigh 175 pounds and there are a dozen different ways of proving those facts. It is no less true to say that after sixty years of marriage, Jacqui and I still love each other deeply. But no laboratory in the world can prove or disprove our affections. The converse applies: you do not have to prove something scientifically for it to be true.

I believe that the approach to near-death experiences should be spiritual not medical. Secular scientists claim we are binary, composed of body and soul (or, if you prefer, body and mind). They claim that when the body dies, the soul dies with it.

In contrast, theologians say we are composed of body, soul and spirit and that death occurs when the spirit leaves the body. That is the view which the Greek philosophers taught

2,500 years ago. It is also how the bible describes death: 'The body without the spirit is dead' (James 2:26).

In the theological paradigm the spirit may leave a body when it is *in extremis*, undergo various experiences, re-enter the body and resume life. During its absence the brain may act as a radio receiver of external impulses, and not simply a creator of consciousness.

That would explain the astonishing finding that in a near-death experience blind people (including those who have been blind from birth) can 'see.' They will later describe people, objects and events in an operating theatre or at the scene of an accident as accurately as if they were normally sighted. These are facts for which there is simply no scientific explanation.

It is wrong to try to explain away near-death experiences medically, and to regard those who have them as drugged or deluded. They need to have their accounts affirmed and explained. Let me restate the point I made earlier: 'Just because you can't explain a thing doesn't mean it's not true.'

Much about near-death experiences remains controversial and I do not presume to know all the answers. But one thing is sure: if they are true and there is something beyond the grave, they are a huge riposte to humanistic teaching. You might argue that they are a dress rehearsal for the real thing, i.e. when you die, you embark on a journey that may end in paradise or somewhere quite different.

Different? Yes, because a minority of subjects have experiences of a negative kind. At best they are distressing and at worst terrifying. Any spiritual beings that they meet are evil. There appears to be no constant link between a negative experience and atheism, a bad life, depression or attempted suicide. Some researchers believe that, in the long-run, negative experiences turn out positive because they cause people to re-evaluate how they live and to make changes. By this rule a negative experience is incomplete; the subject simply needs time to process it in order to benefit from it.

You can appreciate from this account that near-death experiences have influenced my thinking about life and death.

They made even more sense when I was able to put them into the context of Christian faith.

Let me end the chapter on a different note. Not all people take these matters seriously. They find them weird, even absurd. The waters have been muddied by people who dabble in psychic phenomena, time warps and astral travel.

One man on a P&O cruise brought the house down during the question time at the end of my talk. Our exchange went like this:

'Doctor, do people ever have more than one near-death experience?'

'Yes, they may have two but only rarely.'

'Well, I've had dozens!'

'Really? Under what circumstances?'

'They happen on a Friday night.'

I should have ignored the man and turned to the next questioner. But foolishly I asked, 'Why on Friday?'

'That's when me and the missus make love.'

12

Rites of Passage

Throughout my time at Salisbury we lived in a house in Downton, a sprawling village which has nothing to do with the fictional Downton Abbey. The house was aptly named The Warren. It had nine bedrooms, a library, an oak-panelled dining room and bell-pulls to summon servants. The place once belonged to the bishops of Winchester and oozed mediaeval charm. There was woodworm everywhere, even in the toilet seats. That apart, it was paradise after our basement flat behind Victoria Station.

The owner was Dr Tom Hughes-Jones, a consultant paediatrician who was about to go overseas to work for a children's charity. 'All I want is a safe pair of hands to look after the place and keep it free of damp,' he said. 'How about four pounds a week? You'll have to keep the domestic help. My wife will need them when we get back.'

We struck a gentleman's agreement and shook hands on it. Jacqui inherited two charladies at ten shillings an hour. The rent was vastly exceeded by the Warren's mammoth heating bills.

After finishing at the Salisbury infirmary in mid-summer, I had time on my hands. I was on gardening leave, waiting for the RAF's introductory course for new medical officers to begin. It had no use for me until then, so I enjoyed a season of refreshment and fun with my family. It was the lull before the storm.

For the first time in six years, I enjoyed something like a normal family life. At the rear of the house was a large garden surrounded by an ancient wall. In spring Jacqui planted potatoes, artichokes, shallots and runner beans. In summer Rob and Kate, now seven and three, dashed around the lawn with few clothes on, playing happily with our latest acquisition, an Irish setter puppy. The New Forest was minutes away. We explored its heaths, picnicked in its glades and, when we could find them, marvelled at the ponies and the deer.

The Warren was a great house in which to entertain, and we had a stream of visitors. One evening we invited a dozen doctors from the infirmary for a candle-lit dinner. Afterwards we sat around the table drinking wine and telling stories. Then someone produced an *ouija* board and the nonsense started. 'Is there anybody in the room tonight?'

Personally, I never considered that kind of activity healthy and today I would not countenance it. The room was on a half-landing and its oak panels, creaking floorboards and flickering candles inflamed the guests' imagination. As their excitement increased I became irritated. I slipped out into the garden, put a nylon stocking over my head and placed a ladder against the wall. When my distorted face appeared at the window uttering bloodcurdling moans, strong men yelled and women swooned. The *ouija* board went back in the box and the party broke up not long afterwards.

* * *

During this time I made an important discovery about myself. Oliver Goldsmith's poem *The Deserted Village* describes the influence that a saintly preacher had upon the villagers in his congregation. It includes the haunting line, 'And fools, who came to scoff, remained to pray.' That line struck me personally. I had come to medicine late in life not to scoff, but with little real passion for the subject. It was an end to a means.

Twelve months as a houseman forced me to reflect on my position. I realised that I no longer wanted simply to write about medicine; I wanted to practise it. To say that I had fallen in love with doctoring would be too grand, but to my surprise, and notwithstanding all the tribulations, I discovered a genuine compassion for the sick, a desire to heal and above all a fascination with diseases. In a word, like Goldsmith's yokels, I stayed to pray.

Writing remained important and I have never abandoned it, but medicine was now my metier and writing was a recreation. Anton Chekhov had a metaphor for this. He described medicine as his lawful wife and literature as his mistress. He wrote, 'When I get fed up with one, I spend the night with the other. Though it is irregular it is less boring this way, and besides, neither of them loses anything through my infidelity.'

First, I had to pay the piper and serve five years as a medical officer (MO) on an RAF station. That meant general practice with special responsibilities for aircrew, and it meant undergoing training in aviation medicine. The prospect did not deter me. The medical branches of all three services had good reputations and at the time I felt that I would probably end up as a family doctor, like my father and grandfather.

Not all young doctors felt that way. In the 1960s most medical students dreamed of becoming hospital specialists. Hospitals were the sharp end of the profession where the fame and riches lay. General practice was barely a specialty in its own right; it was more a cottage industry, albeit one in which most doctors ended up.

There was a great deal of jealousy between the two wings of the profession and Lord Moran, the president of the Royal College of Physicians, did not help the situation. When seeking to justify the substantial merit awards which consultants received and GPs did not, he described the latter as 'failed consultants' who had 'fallen off the ladder.' He should have known better.

The slur was wholly unmerited, and it infuriated the GPs. But actually, they were living in a glass house and vulnerable to stone throwing. They had no compulsory training programme and there was no way of assessing their competence. New entrants decided for themselves whether or not to take postgraduate training in subjects like child health and obstetrics. The fledglings determined when they were ready to fly.

One consequence of the gulf between specialists and GPs was that house officers with a hospital mindset judged the latter harshly. They were resentful when a GP pulled a fast one and dumped a problem patient on them. (They still are.) My friend John Barr was on duty at a hospital in Billericay in Essex one evening when he had to admit an elderly man.

The referral note was brief. 'Acute urinary retention, patient distressed. On examination: BPH. Impossible to catheterize, needs supra-pubic drain. Thanks for taking him.'

When the patient arrived on the ward, he was indeed distressed; his bladder was the size of a watermelon. (BPH is shorthand for benign enlargement of the prostate gland.) To John's astonishment, a urinary catheter had been correctly inserted and dangled between the patient's legs like a dog's lead. Whoever introduced it had also pushed a spigot into the tube to prevent urine flowing everywhere. The moment it was removed, urine gushed out with the velocity of a howitzer.

John described the incident over a pint of beer. 'It was a complete cock-up. The GP, lazy beggar, probably never spoke to the district nurse and she probably had no collecting bag. One thing is certain; he never saw the patient. He simply lifted the phone.'

John was destined for the Royal Army Medical Corps and knew how to speak bluntly. He waited until the small hours before waking the GP and informing him that he was an arse. The GP was outraged. 'Young man, how dare you address me like that! I have been practising medicine for twenty-five years. I shall report you ...'

'Don't mean a thing, chum. Twenty-five times eff-all is still eff-all. G'night.'

* * *

In September 1970 my orders came to report to RAF Henlow to be introduced to Service life. The course was known officially as the Professionally Qualified and Re-Entrants' Course, and popularly as the Old Peculiars and Re-Treads. We were a group of twenty doctors and nurses, and an engineer who was rejoining the Service. One of the nurses was a little gullible. We kidded her that the RAF motto *Per Ardua ad Astra* meant 'after work we go to the cinema.' It was an old joke but it worked.

Our instructors taught us a great deal in a short time but not all of it stuck, particularly how to deal with the paperwork. The RAF has a bewildering array of forms called FMeds, which are used for everything from keeping a serviceman's medical record (FMed 4) to certifying a pregnancy (FMed 790) and examining a captured prisoner of war (FMed 1026). The military jargon and the abbreviations that went with them were an impenetrable thicket.

Halfway through the process we were given a booklet that suggested that we were being groomed for a different planet. It was called *Customs and Traditions of the Royal Air Force*. The Service had started life in 1918 with neither, but over the course of fifty years it had acquired a hangar full of them. There were columns on how to wear a sword correctly, how to salute on horseback and who could fly a flag on their car. I was surprised to learn that it was illegal for an officer in uniform to carry a parcel in public.

The information we received about an officers' mess was especially revealing. Apparently, it was far more than a club with subsidized alcohol. Everything of social importance happened there: cocktail parties, formal dinners, musical soirées, balls, lectures, film evenings and so on. It was where you exchanged gossip, ideas, jokes and complaints. For young officers it was a testing ground for positions of responsibility. That seemed to be done by strictly enforcing the mess rules on dress and behaviour and by capping their bar bills.

Mess nights were regarded as parades, and you attended them in full mess kit with medals. The mess silver was out on show, the stewards wore white gloves and a military band played airs in a side room. You did not discuss religion or politics and no gentleman dreamed of mentioning what he paid his tailor. If you wanted to take a leak during dinner, you approached the President of the Mess Committee for permission and risked becoming an object of scorn.

Alternatively (so I was told) in some messes you waited for a signal. The President would rise, stand momentarily, and sit again, after which you were free to head for the toilet. This ritual may have been a symbolic act of urination, but I never saw it performed so it was probably a leg pull.

If you were lucky, the President of the Mess Committee did not possess the strongest bladder in the house, and he led the way. That allowed others to follow.

When you were posted to a new station, you were expected to call upon the wife of the commanding officer (CO). The trick was to do it when she was not at home, since introducing yourself on the doorstep was a commercial traveller's trick. You left a visiting card with the maid. If you were favoured, you received a formal invitation to tea the next week.

Junior officers were at a disadvantage in several ways. They might marry without their CO's permission (this was a recent concession) but they were not eligible for married quarters. Nor did they receive the marriage allowance until the age of 25.

Tick-tock, tick-tock ... Keep in ******* step!!

The course had moments of hilarity, notably on the parade ground. We were required to drill like other personnel and the nurses were hopeless at it. They kept in step for no more than three paces. Some of them moved their left arm and leg together and their right arm and leg together, a form of locomotion called 'tick-tocking.' It drove the drill instructor mad. He was a warrant officer with cadaveric features known as the Screaming Skull.

When learning to salute, the nurses' efforts resembled the waves of a drowning swimmer trying to attract attention. A crowd of airmen would gather and wave back until the Skull bawled them away. His scatological language reduced the nurses to tears and we were glad to see the back of him, as no doubt he was of us.

We visited various specialist medical units. An RAF station in Rutland had a decompression chamber in which aircrew were trained how to use partial pressure suits, which prevented them losing consciousness if cabin pressure was lost. The highlight of our visit was undergoing that dubious pleasure.

We 'ascended' to 35,000 feet while inhaling pressurized oxygen through a mask. The temperature at that altitude is normally -55°C, but they held it at -10°C. A freezing mist formed on my visor and strange things began to happen in my body. As the chamber pressure fell, bubbles of expanding air forced their way from my innards (now a high-pressure zone) to the outside world, like a whale expelling air through its blowhole. I would never have believed myself capable of a 20-second fart, but I produced one that day and was mightily relieved to do so. How fighter pilots managed to fly jets at the same time I could not imagine.

The Old Peculiars' course lasted nine weeks before we received our postings. In 1970 Britain had lost most of her Empire. A chap could still join the Royal Navy and see the world, but if he joined the RAF he was more likely to end up in East Anglia.

The individual at the Air Ministry who arranged postings had a perverse sense of humour. Those who volunteered to go overseas got home postings, while those who wanted to stay at home went overseas. I asked for overseas, hoping for somewhere sunny and exotic. I got Shropshire.

13

Station Medical Officer

Tern Hill is a village in Shropshire, seventeen miles north of Shrewsbury and thirty miles east of Wales. It lies in one of the most tranquil parts of England, or so I thought until I arrived there. RAF Tern Hill at the time was the Service's training school for helicopter pilots.

The school had received a new intake of students, and several helicopters were practising take-offs and landings around the grass airfield. The air was filled with thunder, and I had to grip my ears as well as my Service cap.

'Noisy beggars aren't they?' laughed Dai Davis, the station education officer who showed me round. 'You'll soon get used to them.'

The Sioux choppers were versatile creatures, but they were no beauties. They had a bubble-shaped canopy, a fuselage like a bird cage and runners like giant skis. The early versions flew in the Korean War and would be familiar to viewers of *MASH*.

'We call 'em flying egg whisks,' said Dai. 'They're tough but not indestructible. Let me show you something.' He led the way to a hangar and pushed back a huge door. The remains of two helicopters lay scattered on the floor like Meccano sets. Several airmen were on their knees counting the pieces.

'They collided during an exercise. One was taking off and the other landing and wham! – they met halfway. Luckily they were at no great height and fell into a ploughed field. No one was hurt. You missed the action by a week.'

My friend John Kershaw (who like me later trained as an RAF pathologist) did not miss the action when he was posted to RAF Valley in Anglesey; he flew headlong into it. In the first week a wife-swapping circle on the married patch blew up, with two suicide attempts. Tragically one of them was successful.

John told me, 'A host of senior officers descended on the station. I thought they were there to help but all they wanted to do was to keep the lid on everything and kill the publicity. I could barely find my way round the medical centre, never mind anywhere else. I was of no use to anyone.'

The next week things got worse. An RAF Gnat suffered a bird strike on take-off and flew into the sea, killing the pilot who was unable to eject. More senior officers and gold braid descended.

Back to Tern Hill and more positive things. The facilities I was given would have turned the average GP green with envy. The medical centre employed a flight sergeant with a dozen airmen and women as orderlies and clerks. It had a ward, a pharmacy, a small operating theatre, a dispensary and a room for lab tests. It had a civilian nurse for the families, a Mini for making home visits and its own ambulance for emergencies.

All this was for a few hundred men with their wives and children, so we were hardly stretched. In addition to general doctoring, I had to take special care of the aircrew. I was issued with a helmet and flying suit to accompany them on exercises but rarely used them. Instead, I attended crash practices and fire drills on the ground. They were far less exciting.

I was allocated married quarters on the station, a sizeable detached house which was above my entitlement as a flight lieutenant. Each quarter had a fruiting cherry tree in the front garden, but we did not stay long enough to taste the cherries.

That Christmas was the first I spent with my family in three years. I was single-handed and continuously on call. The RAF was paranoid about keeping an MO on duty whether flying was going or not. I could not leave the station because we had no long-distance bleepers. Cell phones lay in the future.

Snow started to fall on Christmas Eve and continued for days. The station threw a children's party with a mammoth tea, a film show, puppets and games. Santa Claus arrived by helicopter, scattering presents from fifty feet up in the air before coming down the cable. His dramatic arrival, albeit without reindeer, restored Rob's faith in the myth.

But seasonal good will did not last long. The weather was bitter, and the coal miners took the opportunity to strike and plunge Britain into misery. We soon ran out of candles and paraffin. The postal workers and telephonists also went on strike for seven weeks.

Meanwhile I was discovering the truth about doctoring on a small station in a corner of England in peacetime. Most of my patients had social rather than medical problems. They were airmen dodging duties or wanting to get booted out of the Service. The aircrew were selected for their fitness and their commonest complaint was haemorrhoids. The chief need among married men was for vasectomies.

The wives' problems were marital, and they wanted to share more of them than I wanted to hear. It seemed there was little to do except procreate and they always brought their kids along to the medical centre. Day after day I cauterized warts, syringed ears and eradicated threadworms.

Like John Kershaw I too inherited a wife-swapping circle, but mercifully it did not end in a suicide. Training Command dealt with it summarily by dispersing the guilty parties with their wives to several different stations. This presumably spread the problem a good deal wider.

I had few ill or elderly patients. There were some diabetic wives who were well controlled, a few epileptics and a small amount of heart disease. Every week I dusted off the coronary crash trolley in the sick quarters and taught someone new to use it, but we never used it in earnest.

I began to worry that if I stayed as an MO on a station – certainly on *that* station – I would forget most of the medicine I had learned.

Boredom was infectious. An admin officer yawned so widely during a lecture that he dislocated his jaw. I had to refer him for the joint to be wired up and for weeks he fed through a straw. Whenever I saw him around the station I thought, 'There but for the grace of God.'

The philosopher Henry Thoreau wrote that our lives are consumed with trifles. Mine was consumed with sick parades, vaccination parades, annual examinations, antenatal clinics, postnatal clinics and hygiene inspections. And I had no way of knowing if I did them competently.

But life was not all routine. My peace was broken by an airman who behaved normally at work and terrorized his wife at home in their quarters. She worked as a waitress in the officers' mess and approached me there, for she was too scared to attend the medical centre. Things went from bad to worse and he took to slitting her dresses with a razor. It was unarguably psychotic behaviour and I had him admitted urgently to the RAF's acute psychiatric unit. I advised the wife to go back to her parents for a spell. She did so, but months later her husband tracked her down and knifed her to death. I learned of her death after I had left Tern Hill. I felt physically sick and racked my brains for what else I might have done. I could think of nothing. There are some scenarios which are not taught when you are a student.

* * *

News came through that the station was getting a senior medical officer. That stopped me making a hurried decision. I resolved to wait to see what difference he made to my situation.

The new arrival, whom I shall call Wing Commander Freddie Martin, was in his fifties. He had the most bombastic presence of any doctor I ever met. He was half French and stockily built with a thick moustache and fierce brown eyes. During World War II he was parachuted into France to work with the Resistance. He wore a dog whistle round his neck and a chestful of ribbons sewn onto an obsolete battledress blouse, thus committing two offences against the uniform code. He was passionate about field sports and was accompanied everywhere by two black labradors.

Freddie was the oldest wing commander in the medical branch. Of course, this was not the kind of distinction a man sought; it meant that he had been repeatedly passed over for promotion. He had been an anaesthetist for many years and by all accounts was a good one, but he refused to sit the examinations of the Royal College of Anaesthetists which were essential for promotion to consultant.

His argument and his language (which was colourful) were along these lines: 'If I'm good enough at gassing without having effing letters after my name, why should I take a test to please some effing pen pusher?'

After years of arguing with him, the medical branch lost patience and transferred him to hospital administration. Being kicked out of the specialty which he loved did nothing to improve his temper.

I did not realise at first that Freddie was more than just unconventional; he was a genuine eccentric. Years later I studied eccentricity and gave talks about it on cruise ships. There is a small but interesting body of medical literature on the subject. Eccentrics lead such chaotic lives that they find it difficult to hold down regular employment, particularly a demanding job like medicine.

Freddie was an exception, but his life ran narrowly short of chaos. He survived in a military system because he was good at what he did, and the air crews loved him. He had 'bottom' or derring-do courage (another mark of the eccentric), and the medals to go with it.

Like most eccentrics he was a collector. Over the years he gassed at hundreds of dental extractions. He harvested the teeth and had them polished, drilled and made into an ivory necklace. I saw a photograph of him wearing it over green theatre scrubs. He looked like a cannibal at a party.

At Tern Hill he and his wife moved into married quarters, and on the first day he spotted a pheasant perching on the garden fence. Having initially sent in his dog to make it rise, he then shot it from the back door. Later he insisted that this justified the act, since a sportsman's first rule is, 'Never shoot a sitting bird.' It didn't matter to him that it was a serious offence to keep a weapon in married quarters, rather than in the station armoury. Let alone discharge it.

The wife of an air vice-marshal lived in an official residence nearby and she was not pleased. The bird turned out to be half-domesticated and she fed it by hand. Like the Ancient Mariner who shot an albatross (not a pheasant), Freddie would suffer for the offence.

Soon after his arrival, I was detached to cover RAF Hereford, a World War II station which was later taken over by the army. It had a hospital with over 100 beds, operating theatres, a radiology department, a gymnasium and other facilities. I was in sole charge and walked its echoing corridors.

I had one in-patient, a soldier from the Special Air Service whose headquarters were nearby. His skin was sallow, his breathing laboured, and his temperature rose steadily. In these circumstances a doctor must ask a critical question.

'Where have you been recently?'

The soldier's eyes rolled. In his feverish state he probably took me for a KGB interrogator. 'Jenkins, trooper, 79546, suh!'

I tried several times and got the same answer. The man stuck to standing orders and divulged nothing.

We identified malarial parasites in his blood and packed him off to an army hospital. I later learned he had been on covert operations in the Middle East. In other circumstances his adherence to the rule book might have cost him his life.

That small triumph was followed by an officer cadet from a Gulf state, who complained in broken English of 'leetle aneemuls in zee eyes.' His eyes were healthy enough, but the roots of his eyelashes were crawling with lice. I started him on treatment. At sick parade the next day two more cadets showed up. They had the same problem.

At this point I must point out the *pediculosis capitis*, or head lice, are a different type from *pediculosis pubis* or pubic lice, vulgarly known as the crabs. Head lice are rare in healthy adults and not normally regarded as sexually transmitted. Either these lads shared the same hairbrush, or they had some outlandish leisure activities.

Back at RAF Tern Hill, Freddie's gun dogs had taken up residence under his desk and growled if anyone approached when he was behind it. The airmen's wives insisted on being seen by me. This led to friction, as did Freddie's conduct when he made visits on the airmen's patch. He would wind down the car window, bang the door and sound the horn while yelling, 'Get up you lazy so-and-sos, the doctor's here!'

Because of Freddie's blustering ways I struggled with the rank system. The theory is that when you salute a superior officer you show respect to the rank rather than to the individual. That lets your conscience off the hook if he behaves like an idiot. Freddie was far from being an idiot, but I frequently disagreed with his judgments and was obliged to obey him. It was not an easy partnership.

I thought of myself as a caring doctor, but two events around this time shocked me. One day I was examining a lady who complained of a host of vague symptoms. I was not actually listening to her nor was I examining her properly. It was late in the afternoon; the daylight was fading and so was my compassion. I could only think of one thing, 'How do I get rid of this confounded woman?'

Then I remembered something we were taught as students: all neurotics have to die of something at some time. That thought kept me on the straight and narrow path.

On another occasion I attended a dining-in night after a long day. I made my excuses and left the mess as soon as I decently could. Around midnight I was fast asleep when the phone rang. A slurred voice said, 'Hey doc, you're needed back here. Bring your bag. There's been a bit of a to-do.'

An aging wing commander on the administrative staff was slumped on the floor in the bar, his shirt front covered in blood and his thinning hair dishevelled. He had been playing horses-and-riders with men half his age and broken glass lay around. His waistcoat and mess jacket were discarded. He was exceedingly drunk and generally a disgrace to his uniform.

He had a deep cut on his scalp. I did not ask how it happened and said through gritted teeth, 'You need stitching. You don't want a local, do you?'

'Nah, you go ahead, doc. Do what you gotta do.'

Empathy went out of the window. I sloshed surgical spirit over his wound and jabbed in the needle as if I were gaffing a salmon. He was going to learn from this folly.

In retrospect I am not proud of my attitude, even though I later learned that most doctors have similar lapses. At the time it made me wonder if I was a natural clinician and probably influenced my next career move.

Nonetheless, the wing commander's behaviour was shameful and from then on, I looked the other way if he came within saluting distance. True respect has to be earned.

* * *

I had another problem with the military system. There was a taboo against senior and junior officers socializing except at official functions. That seemed to me nonsensical, and I decided to test it. Jacqui and I invited a group captain and his wife from a neighbouring station to dinner. They were both my patients and delightful people. It may have been inappropriate for a junior MO, but I asked them anyway and they accepted.

The day arrived and Jacqui cooked her speciality dish, which was a roast shoulder of lamb with rosemary and garlic stuffed into the incisions, served with lots of vegetables and lashings of gravy. She put the joint to rest on the kitchen table and joined us for drinks in the sitting room. After she left to make the final touches, she did not return. I served another round. Ten minutes passed. I suggested more drinks and the guests declined. I excused myself and hurried to the kitchen.

'What on earth's going on?!'

Jacqui was distraught. She whacked the joint with a rolling pin like a deranged panel beater.

'Don't ask! Just get them into the dining room and carve this bloody thing.'

The rest of the evening passed off smoothly and we had an excellent meal. Two years later at a different station I met the group captain's wife again. She recalled the evening with great pleasure, and I then revealed the truth. Our Irish setter bitch, Jade, was well advanced in pregnancy and living in a whelping box in the kitchen. I had fashioned it out of a tea chest and nailed a piece of carpet over the front to give her darkness and quiet. I was pretty pleased with the result; we called it the labour ward.

When Jacqui returned to the kitchen, the joint had vanished. A trail of gravy led to the tea chest and when the curtain was twitched there were deep growls from within. It took five minutes to recover our dinner, beat out the teeth marks and re-baste it.

The group captain's wife roared with laughter. 'I thought there was something wrong,' she said, 'but I decided it was a case of young hostess nerves.'

In mitigation of the offence, Jade whelped the next day and delivered ten beautiful red pups, twice as many as the local vet predicted. Freddie Martin proved to a first class veterinary *accoucheur*. The kitchen was filled with RAF kids marvelling at the deliveries.

I had grown fond of Freddie, but it was clear that the RAF had dumped him permanently at Tern Hill. He had hit the end of the runway; there was no way he would move from there. The thought that I might be yoked to him for years was more than I could stand.

I had to get away, but where? Certainly not to another flying station. The answer was to an RAF hospital, of which there were six in the UK and three overseas. They were often on the look-out for trainees, but I had been told there were no vacancies. Then out of the blue a circular letter arrived, asking if any junior MO was interested in becoming a pathologist. I thought long and hard and talked it through with Jacqui, then sat down and wrote an application.

You may be pardoned for considering me fickle. After a good start in technical journalism, I abandoned it with what might seem untimely haste. I wriggled my way into the Middlesex in order to become a medical writer and gave up that idea after qualifying. I convinced myself that I wanted to care for patients. When that did not turn out as I wished, I turned to pathology.

But I was no gadfly. In my youth I was always torn between two poles. At Oxford I followed the arts, at the Middlesex I followed science, and at *The Times* I combined them. I could wear either glove with comfort. The question was: which was the better fit?

With regard to clinical medicine, I inherited the idea from my father and grandfather that a general practitioner was far more than a medic. The model that I admired was drawn not from AJ Cronin or *Dr Finlay's Casebook*, but from the novelist and poet John Berger. He wrote one of the most influential books to date about general practice. It was recommended reading for trainees. I lapped it up.

A Fortunate Man: the Story of a Country Doctor tells of Dr John Eskell, a single-handed GP in the Forest of Dean. It explores the emotional as well as the professional relationship between a GP and his patients. Eskell was their friend, confidant and champion. He cared for them from birth to death, sharing their joys and their misfortunes.

That approach to medicine has long since vanished. It was destroyed by changes in the NHS and in medical practice itself. Nor was it sustainable; the price paid by GPs in exhaustion, depression and marital breakdown was too high. The suicide rate has always been high among doctors; Eskell took his own life at the age of 63.

It was foolish of me to think that Eskell's ideal (or something like it) might apply in the military. Conditions there are different. Medical officers do things by the book. They are authority figures, which sets them apart and makes friendships with patients hard to forge. They are birds of passage and rarely stay in one place for long. Their subordination to a non-medical CO often conflicts with their conscience as physicians.

I found it hard to accept all this. If you take into account the lack of real medicine and my difficulties with my boss, my change of heart may not look so opportunistic.

Freddie snorted when he heard about the pathology training scheme. 'Son, you may think it's noble to dedicate yourself to corpses, but why waste six years at medical school? You might as well be an effing undertaker.'

He was upset of course. I was going to join the hospital cadre which had booted him out. And my departure was a kind of desertion; it would leave him in sole charge and drastically reduce his leisurely afternoons spent shooting.

When I last heard of him, the RAF had left Tern Hill. Instead of doing things by the book, which meant returning everything of value to Training Command and writing off the rest, Freddie passed certain medical supplies to a local chemist. Cash changed hands and he was charged with theft on five counts. He came before Shrewsbury Crown Court where happily he was found not guilty. Apparently, the proceeds had gone towards RAF staff benefits and a benevolent fund. He was even awarded costs.

I was glad things did not go the other way. Heaven knows what the prison officers would have made of him.

14

Pathology Training

In the spring of 1971, I was posted to RAF Halton for pathology training. Halton is situated on the edge of the Vale of Aylesbury and just below the escarpment of the Chiltern Hills, in what Benjamin Disraeli called his 'beloved beechy Buckinghamshire.'

At the time it was the largest air force station in the UK. Its technical training school housed some 2,000 engineering apprentices who were affectionately known as Trenchard's brats. It also contained the RAF's leading hospital, its central laboratories and other medical training units.

I use the past tense because the apprentice lads are long gone, the medical buildings have been flattened and the station is facing closure. Already developers have devoured much of it.

The station had a colourful past, as I learned when I came to write a book about it a few years later. Air Vice-Marshal John Cooke, the RAF's senior physician, knew it of old. He first saw the place in 1935 as a teenager when his father was posted there.

Over a drink he told me about those days. 'Between the world wars the RAF was the best flying club in the world. My father's friends kept their private Tiger Moths and Puss Moths in canvas hangars which were left over from the 1914 war. They were always flying off to house parties and sporting events. They regularly buzzed the homes of their girl friends.'

'Did you fly?' I asked.

'I wanted to, but my eyesight wasn't good enough so I took up medicine. But there was other fun at Halton. The place was horse-mad. You could keep a horse and an airman groom on £1 a week. There was hunting, point-to-points, steeple chases and what the airmen called 'orse 'ockey.'

He chuckled. 'That was polo. They loathed us for it. There were chukkas every week on the airfield and 1,000 airmen were marched up and down to flatten the turf. It was only used for polo and ceremonial parades.'

Horse-mad at Halton

He told me about the RAF Princess Mary's Hospital, which dated from the 1920s. 'Our brightest clinicians worked here, and it was a mecca for military medicine. Between the wars it treated all the RAF's venereal diseases; a posting to RAF Halton was a euphemism for something worse. If you got a genuine posting there, you made it very clear to your friends.'

Halton was the first military hospital to use penicillin on a large scale, so any airman who got gonorrhoea was in good hands.

In the days of the British Raj, all the Armed Forces needed experts in tropical medicine. Servicemen returning from the East brought back everything from dengue fever to giant tape worms. The RAF's solution was the awkwardly named Institute of Pathology and Tropical Medicine (IPTM) which grew up alongside the hospital. The glass cabinets in its museum were filled with jars of pickled tarantulas and deadly snakes.

The Institute ran an introductory course for trainees that lasted a year. We got a good grounding in the big four: the sub-specialties of haematology, chemical pathology, microbiology and histopathology. It was the era of the generalist, and pathologists outside the big city hospitals had to be competent in all four disciplines. In the RAF we were also required to become expert in one of them. There would be no copying Freddie Martin and dodging the examinations of our Royal College.

Each sub-specialty seemed to me to have its own attractions. The haematologists were the film stars of the day; they were clinicians as well as scientists, having one foot in the laboratory and the other on the wards. They treated a wide range of diseases including lymphomas and leukaemias and they collaborated with other cancer specialists. The Medical Research Council seemed to shower them with grants.

Microbiology (which combines bacteriology and virology) was a softer option. There was limited patient contact, and the work was neither messy nor especially arduous. Because it involves growing organisms on culture plates, it was often known as 'indoor gardening' and was an attractive option for lady pathologists.

The optimists believed that medicine had already got the better of infectious diseases, and that microbiology would gradually decrease in importance. Nobody foresaw the rise of bacterial drug-resistance and viral pandemics which would project microbiologists to the forefront of the profession.

Chemical pathology was for the boffins. Also known as clinical biochemistry, it is the chemical investigation of body fluids like blood, urine and cerebrospinal fluid. The tests it used were based on colour reactions and required an astonishing range of glassware: test tubes, beakers, retorts, pipettes, graduated cylinders and evaporating dishes. If you include mortars, pestles and Bunsen burners, a chem. path.

bench resembled a cooking lesson conducted by a mad professor. The lab techs did the manual work while the pathologists interpreted the findings, arrived at a diagnosis and monitored the treatment. They enjoyed some patient contact and were constantly enlarging the boundaries of their specialty. (Today the laboratory is dominated by sleek computerized multi-channel analysers which cost a fortune but have replaced many technicians.)

Lastly there was histopathology, the study and diagnosis of diseases at the cellular level using a light microscope. I say lastly because it was not the most popular choice for trainees, since histopathologists were normally tasked with doing all the hospital's post-mortem work. Other pathologists called it a dead-end job. Nevertheless, this is the specialty which I adopted, and I shall leave further details to a later chapter.

During the training course at IPTM, I was introduced to the RAF's Department of Aviation Pathology, which handled the medical investigation of military and civilian fatal aircraft accidents. I attended several crash sites and the post-mortem examinations that followed, including the Staines air disaster described in my first chapter. Now is the time to return to it.

After the process of identifying the dead has been completed, the pathologist's next task is to reconstruct the accident, if he can, on the basis of the pattern of injuries and other post-mortem findings. This is where the story behind the Staines disaster becomes grimly fascinating. The RAF made a significant contribution to it. Two of my senior colleagues, Group Captain Ken Mason and Squadron Leader Tony Cullen gave evidence to the enquiry, as did Air Vice-Marshal Paddy O'Connor, the RAF's senior neuro-psychiatrist. So did several distinguished cardiologists, including Dr Walter Somerville, the Middlesex Hospital consultant whose clerk I had been four years earlier.

After many months, a board of enquiry concluded that the disaster was caused by a pilot error which resulted in the catastrophic stalling of the aircraft. Behind that conclusion was a debate regarding the health of the pilot, Captain Stanley Key, who was 51 years old and a former World War II pilot. The post-mortem examination revealed significant hardening of his coronary arteries. Whatever else, he was not physically fit to fly, though there was no way of knowing that on the day.

The examination also revealed a small tear in the lining of one of the arteries. It was fresh and may have been caused by a rise in his blood pressure during a dispute with other crew members. A heated argument was known to have taken place concerning their pay and conditions shortly before they embarked on the aircraft.

The tear may have caused Captain Key pain and distracted him at a critical moment. A voice recorder in the cockpit would have provided crucial information but recorders were not mandatory and there was none on the Trident. After Staines the rules were changed.

So the question boiled down to this: were the deaths of 118 people attributable in part to that tiny lesion, or was it an incidental finding? The matter had huge significance for the families and for the airline, not least in terms of financial compensation. But as so often happens in post-mortem work, an absolute answer was not possible.

I also acquired some experience of light aircraft accidents. In the summer of 1971, I accompanied Group Captain Ken Mason to the scene of a double fatality in Hampshire. It brought back memories of the weekend conference in Portsmouth, when Peter Stevens presented the factors that conspire to cause disaster. They include poor planning, failure to file a flight plan, forgetting to check fuel tanks, changes in the weather, technical incompetence, flying too low and the Icarus syndrome.

This accident demonstrated several of those factors. One day in August two young men took off from a private airfield in Hampshire that belonged to a gliding club. They were in a single-engine Piper Cub that was normally used as a glider tug and had no radio or blind flying instruments. The passenger was the 21-year-old son of Michael Bentine, the well-known comedian and founding member of the much-loved *Goon Show*. That fact guaranteed headline news during the following months.

The gliding club kept no log of air movements, and the pilot did not file a flight plan or tell anyone where he was going. None of this was illegal but it shows how relaxed private flying was in those days. What was more, two days elapsed before the plane was reported missing.

It was thought that the men were heading for the Solent to take aerial photographs of the powerboat race around the Isle of Wight, being held on that day. Searchers concentrated on their likely route and flew back and forth over the South Downs as far as Chesil Beach.

The days of agony for the families lengthened into weeks and months. What on earth had happened? It seemed impossible that a plane could crash in daylight in southern England and not be found. Could it have flown out to sea and crashed there? But there was no wreckage and no bodies.

More than two months elapsed before a couple walking in woods outside Petersfield spotted the fuselage of the Piper Cub among the trees. When Ken Mason and I arrived it was still standing on its nose, with the decomposed bodies inside. Dense foliage had hidden it from view until the autumn leaves fell. Ken performed the autopsies at a local mortuary, but he could add little to the overall investigation. The airplane had driven vertically into the ground with huge force and the crash was not survivable.

All this exposure to sudden death in the air had an effect on me. After joining the Service I had no desire to gain a RAF medical pilot's wings or a private pilot's licence. In fact, I was less than thrilled about flying in general. Years later Jacqui booked me a flying lesson as a birthday present. Not knowing what was in store, I enjoyed a large Devonshire cream tea an hour before it. I was queasy throughout the flight and politely declined an option to take the full course.

* * *

In January 1972, in the middle of our time at Halton, Jacqui gave birth to our younger daughter Lizby at Princess Mary's Hospital. Like our other children she was delivered by

Caesarean section. Though still a trainee I was the duty blood transfusion officer and it was my job to cross-match four pints of blood. To my horror the tubes coagulated, and I could not obtain a match. The operation could not go ahead without transfusion cover and Jacqui was sent home in tears. A more qualified pathologist took over and I felt an inch high.

The mystery was solved next day when Rob and Kate came out in a measles rash. Jacqui had contracted the disease mildly and without symptoms. The antibodies that troubled me were a harmless consequence of her infection and no reason to defer the delivery, which went ahead smoothly. My self-worth was restored.

That summer, after months of training punctuated by fatal aircraft crashes (which were hardly light relief), I was invited to join an expedition to Arctic Norway as its medical officer. I needed the break. It was selfish to leave Jacqui looking after two youngsters and a baby for six weeks, but she encouraged me to go. My CO approved the idea.

Just before the expedition left, my next posting came through. It was to the RAF Hospital in Ely in Cambridgeshire. There was just time to dash up there and find a house that we both liked. Jacqui then had the considerable task of negotiating its purchase in my absence. She did sterling work with agents and lawyers. The concept of a 'model Service wife' is woefully outdated today, but my generation knew it, and Jacqui excelled in the role.

The expedition was organized by the British Schools Exploring Society and its leaders were drawn from the Armed Forces. The logistics were formidable. I had to arrange for fifty expeditioneers to be vetted medically before they could be accepted, and advise them on their preparations. Without any previous experience I had to organize enough medical supplies to equip a small army for a campaign.

The party went by ship from Newcastle to Bergen before transferring to a coastal steamer. We travelled several days up the Norwegian coast, enjoying spectacular views of the glaciers and mountains. Ours was a working ship which travelled in and out of the fjords, dropping off household goods and picking up fish and farm produce. The crew had little interest in whale sightings and the Northern Lights. Today that journey is a holiday which only the rich can afford.

Our base camp was several hours beyond civilization, in a valley of spruce and pine trees at the head of a fjord. Beyond it the land was wild and forbidding; the Norwegians called it 'the most unwelcoming country.' From a high point you could look over 3,000 square miles of mountains and lakes untouched by human hand. It was Tolkien country. I brought *The Lord of the Rings* with me, and it was just the right kind of reading.

The terrain may have been wild but the doctoring was tame, being restricted to blisters, sprains and sore backs. There were days when I was more a housewife than a medic. The only predators to attack us were biting flies, relatives of the Scottish midges. They were voracious feeders and gathered in clouds dense enough to send a man crazy. My first task – even before the latrines were dug – was to spray the camp with insecticide. Within its boundaries we were partially protected, but whenever we left them we were eaten alive. Goodness knows what the little blighters fed on after we left.

The camp was 100 miles over the Arctic Circle and the weather was hardly what I expected. Captain Scott would have scoffed at our situation. The temperatures were the highest recorded in the Arctic. The snow fields shrank; the lakes rose, and streams became torrents. Trondheim ran out of ice cream.

To persuade the RAF to release me on the expedition, I had devised a research project with Dr Willy Slater, one of my former teachers at the Middlesex Hospital. Willy was a consultant endocrinologist and an expert on the adrenal glands which control the body's response to stress. On paper the expedition offered great opportunities to take samples from young men when they were cold, exhausted and needing sleep. The plan was that Willy would measure the hormone levels in their blood and urine samples and I would correlate them with their blood pressures, pulse rates and stress levels. The results would be ground-breaking and make me famous. (Willy already was famous.)

That was the plan, but things did not work out like that. In the high temperatures the guinea pigs suffered more from sunburn than from cold. The swollen streams curtailed their activities and made it difficult to find their camps. Some lads went down with gastro-enteritis and were ruled out. I found it hard to find ice (in the Arctic!) to preserve the specimens. I failed to get adequate blood samples, but I persevered with the rest of the schedule.

When Oscar Wilde arrived in New York in 1881 he was asked if he had anything to declare. 'Only my genius,' was his alleged reply. When our ship docked in Newcastle I was asked the same question. My answer was less theatrical: 'Only ten gallons of urine.'

And so I came back to RAF Halton. I was bearded, unwashed and unkempt and I carried a set of reindeer antlers on my back. Lizby failed to recognize me on the railway platform and burst into tears.

Now with my family I was about to exchange the Arctic mountains for the Cambridgeshire Fens.

15

Fen Dwellers

The Cambridgeshire Fens are full of curiosities. Chatteris, the market town where we came to live in the autumn of 1972, was once a settlement on the coast. Today it is fifty miles inland and four feet below sea level. Before the Fens were drained in the 17th century, a great part of the land was permanently underwater.

A local saying goes, 'The Fens shrink the height of a man in the life of a man.' Highways which a century ago were level with the fields now stand high above them, like the veins on an old man's hand.

Another curiosity is the Fen Blow. We experienced our first blow while exploring the area by car. One moment we were enjoying the scenery and the next moment a blanket descended and the light disappeared. The car shook and the sky rained pebbles and earth. Someone has likened the experience to driving through Marmite. I stopped and turned on the headlights, and we quaked in our seats until the blow passed.

The explanation is simple. Despite the seasonal flooding, Cambridgeshire has a low rainfall, and a dry spell is followed by gales which dry out the topsoil and whip it into a dust storm. Every year tons of seeds and soil are blown away. Everybody knows that the culprit is intensive farming, but nobody does much about it. And the blows still blow.

We learned the first rule of the Fens, which is never go out and leave your windows open. The peat gets everywhere, into your picture frames, fridges and toothbrushes.

Fen skies are enormous; they extend from one horizon to another and the clouds chase across them like demented sheep. Whichever way you look, the fields seem to stretch to infinity, unbroken by trees and hedges. The locals say you can see next week's weather coming.

In winter, an inland sea opens up between the New Bedford and the Great Ouse rivers, as lovely and tranquil as a Turner painting. Flocks of geese and swans sail on it. Walking there one weekend I came across an old man who had parked his car in the water. He was washing it with a sponge. He gave me a grin. 'Floods is useful if you don't have a standpipe.'

Ely's majestic cathedral, known as the Ship of the Fens, dominates the landscape. In 1939 the RAF built a hospital there to receive casualties from flying stations across East Anglia. It became renowned as a burns unit.

In 1972 wartime relics still remained. A pillbox guarded the gates, softened by a coat of beige over the concrete. Nearby on a plinth stood a beautiful Supermarine Spitfire. When it was requisitioned for a museum and replaced by an ugly jet from the 1950s, there was a furore. The citizens of Ely protested to the Air Ministry: 'We want a proper aeroplane, one with a propeller!'

Over time the brick buildings multiplied and rose to two storeys. When I arrived, the hospital cared for the local population as well as the RAF and was effectively a district hospital. Within the 'exigencies of the Service' (which meant the need not to be swamped by civilians) the GPs had access to the Casualty Department, the surgical and medical beds, the coronary care unit and the obstetric unit. They could also use the physiotherapy, radiology and pathology services.

I was the junior of two pathologists. My boss Charles Newrick was a squadron leader and an experienced practitioner. We had a staff of a dozen qualified technicians, all airmen and airwomen trained by the RAF. We worked happily in one big room divided into separate areas for haematology, chemical pathology and microbiology. The arrangements worked well enough but would not be allowed today.

Laboratories in the 1970s had no computers, automation or mechanical handling. Glass test tubes and Bunsen burners were standard equipment. The tests employed were based on colour reactions and performed manually. You could tell a lab tech at a dozen paces by the stains on his or her fingers.

To measure out an exact quantity of a fluid, you used a mouth pipette: an open-ended tube with calibration marks. Sucking up five millilitres of blood, cerebro-spinal fluid or chemical reagent was risky and unpleasant. Precision pipettes that worked mechanically arrived in the nick of time, just before the AIDS epidemic.

Our contact with infected fluids and chemicals (some of which were carcinogenic, though nobody knew it at the time) took its toll. There was more tuberculosis and hepatitis among laboratory staff in the UK than among any other hospital staff.

Mondays were busy in the Ely lab. We had to clear the weekend backlog and keep up with the clinicians who had a full day of ward rounds, clinics and operations which generated more laboratory work. We also ran an anticoagulant clinic to monitor outpatients' drug dosages.

The anticoagulant patients were mostly elderly and longstanding; they knew each other well and the clinic was like a pensioners' tea party. Nobody complained if they had to wait because we saved them a journey of 25 miles to Addenbrooke's Hospital in Cambridge. RAF Ely was hugely popular and was known as 'our hospital.'

Pathologists seldom get gifts from patients, so it was a red-letter day when an elderly villager presented me with a shopping bag that clinked. It contained brown quart bottles labelled carrot, turnip and beet. The taste was somewhere between sewage and diesel oil. She told me that she collected vegetables that fell off the stalls at the Ely market and were squashed in the gutter. 'I only brews the wine when I can afford the sugar,' she added.

When Jacqui heard the story, she smiled her gentle smile. 'Never mind, darling. It's the thought that counts.'

On another occasion the mother-in-law of the deputy lord-lieutenant of the county died at the start of the salmon season. To oblige him, the hospital CO ordered me to come in at a weekend and perform a post-mortem, so that the gentleman could attend the burial and hurry off to Scotland. A month later half a smoked salmon was delivered to my office. I often wondered if that was gratitude or a retrospective bribe.

The mortuary lay away from prying eyes behind the motor transport pool. It was a stout shed with steel rafters and a corrugated iron roof. It was inspected regularly, like everything on a military base, but it was not heavily used. Servicemen and women are generally fit and not expected to die. The local population kept it in use with road accidents and agricultural accidents.

Road accidents in the Isle of Ely sometimes ended in drowning. I have described how the roads stand high above the level of the fields. If a driver loses control he can slip off and end up in a canal running alongside the road. They are called rhynes and have strange names like Bevill's Leam, New Popham's Eau, Kings Dike and Forty Foot Drain. I was first on the scene of one such accident, which happily did not end in a drowning. After a long evening as orderly medical officer, I set out for home under a full moon. The road ahead of me gleamed like silver. All of a sudden, a ghastly apparition reared up in my path and forced me to brake heavily. It was a man in evening dress, waving frantically. His hair was dishevelled, and his shirt front was drenched with blood. 'Help me for God's sake! My wife's down there ... I can't get her out.' He pointed to the Fen.

I had stopped where a minor road joined from the left. The driver had come up that road, missed the halt sign and shot over the junction. His car had pancaked in a beet field. The engine was dead and the lights out. I clambered down a bank and opened the passenger door. Inside a woman was moaning, 'I can't see, I can't see!' Her face was bloody and covered in glass from the windscreen.

She was not petite, and it took all my strength to carry her across the field and up the bank. On the journey back to Ely I learned that the couple had recently arrived in the area and had been attending a social event near Cambridge. That explained the evening dress.

A ghastly apparition reared up before me

Back at the hospital I examined them in the Casualty Department. The man had bruises and scalp wounds which were quickly dressed but his wife had multiple cuts to her eyelids, some of them deep. I feared for her sight. This was no job for a pathologist, so I phoned the junior eye surgeon who was a flight lieutenant.

'Not my problem,' he said sleepily. 'The wing co's your man.'

'Who?'

'Wing Commander John Cloherty. He arrived last week. He's on call tonight.' The phone clicked.

As I prepared to redial, a nurse came in to announce that the bloodstained driver was in fact Ely's new consultant eye surgeon. The flight lieutenant ended up treating his boss and referring his wife Pauline to Addenbrooke's Hospital. Happily, her injuries healed well, and her sight was not affected. In due course I received another gift, a beautiful jade egg.

The hospital commander was Group Captain Rob Covell, a nice fellow if a little officious. I was summoned to his office.

'Andy, I suspect that alcohol may have played a part in the accident.'

'I assure you, sir, I hadn't taken a drop.'

'Don't be facetious! What was your opinion regarding the sobriety of the driver?'

'I really couldn't say, sir. I was busy giving aid to the wounded.'

'Didn't you take blood for alcohol?'

I knew my medico-legal stuff even if he didn't. 'No call for that, sir. Only one vehicle involved and no third-party damage. Only a police surgeon could take blood.'

The Cloherties became good friends to Jacqui and me. John went on to become an air commodore and the RAF's senior eye surgeon.

Another case in which a vehicle landed on the Fen had a different ending. The police report ran like this: 'Van crashed near Soham at 1600 hours. Driver found dead at wheel. No other vehicle involved. Death certified at 1715 hours.'

Those details were barely sufficient, but the case seemed straightforward. Few vehicles in those days had seat belts and fewer drivers bothered with them. I was sure that I would find injuries to the skull, chest or abdomen and possibly all three.

The dead man was in his late twenties and dressed in a donkey jacket, jeans and boots. His face looked puzzled, as if death had caught him unawares. Another surprise came when we undressed him; there were no lacerations, blood, bruises or broken bones. We turned him over. There was nothing to find.

An hour later and with help from my technician, Corporal Clegg, I had extracted the innards without slicing myself. The brain was pristine, the liver healthy and the spleen (which is the most fragile of organs) was undamaged. There was nothing amiss within the abdominal cavity. The thoracic pluck, a weighty dissection comprising the tongue, larynx, mediastinum, lungs and heart was unbruised. In fact everything was in mint condition, untouched by trauma or disease.

With a furrowed brow I fell to opening, dissecting and slicing. This was ridiculous. How could I *not* find an explanation for the man's death? It was not enough to state 'road traffic accident' as the cause. The coroner would not wear that.

The coroner's officer was an affable police constable but his approach to his work was often casual, and I vented my frustration on him. 'Mr Gridley, the report is inadequate! I need details of how the body was found and I need photographs of the van. Today, if you please.'

Five minutes later I was back in the laboratory, trying to catch up on the morning. Lunch was long past.

When Gridley returned, he handed me the police file. The new information ran: 'The van left the road on a corner and struck a tree. Deceased was found with head forced over the wheel. Firemen used cutting gear to remove body.'

There were Polaroid photographs. A partition behind the front seats had buckled under pressure from the cargo. A line of burst rivets was clearly visible. The driver's head had been forced over the top of the steering wheel.

Another photograph showed where the van had come to rest in the field, its bonnet crumpled around something the size of a telephone kiosk. Corporal Clegg peered at it and exclaimed, 'That's a bog oak!' Bog oaks are the remains of giant trees that grew on the Fens for centuries before they were drained. When farmers plough them up, they shift them to the one side if they can.

The mystery was starting to resolve. For some reason – a momentary distraction, a patch of mud or excessive speed – the van had left the road and careered down the bank. It struck the only solid object for miles around.

I took another look at the body. There were pinpoint haemorrhages on the inside of the eyelids that I had missed because I was not looking for them. A fresh dissection with a magnifying glass revealed just enough swelling and distortion in the larynx to show that the vocal cords had been compressed.

The victim did not die from injuries. He died from asphyxia in a cruel and freakish accident. The collapsed partition had trapped his neck over the steering wheel.

At this point Corporal Clegg broke in. 'What was the van carrying, Mr Gridley?'

Gridley consulted the report. 'It says here, a load of frozen fish fingers.'

'Well, there's the answer,' Clegg chortled. 'It was an act of cod!'

The joke may jar with some readers, and I do not wish it to take away from the tragedy of the young man's death. It is an example of how mortuary humour applied to the circumstances of a death (not to the dead person) can release tension. The effect is to make everything a little easier for those present. I shall return to the point in a later chapter.

* * *

Doctors learn as much from their mistakes as their successes and that case taught me not to dive in with preconceived ideas. In a mortuary, as in a laboratory, a pathologist depends on the information given to him and it should be as complete as possible.

Most of the autopsies I performed at Ely were for the coroner, a local solicitor who looked favourably on the hospital and who detested publicity. If an inquest was coming up that was likely to be contentious, he would change the schedule and hold it an hour ahead of the advertised time. When a reporter showed up, he would find the whole matter done and dusted and all he obtained was the bare verdict of the court.

It was a stunt the coroner could not pull too often, but he used it when a middle-aged woman was found dead in her bathroom with a plastic bag over her head. She had suffered for years from muscle weakness and joint pains which were the late effects of polio.

John Dupere, the lady's GP, was a good friend of mine. He found her body and when called to give evidence he brought along the plastic bag. The coroner ignored it and surprised us by asking questions that had nothing to do with her polio or her mental state. Had the deceased ever had chest pain? Was her pulse regular? Was she a smoker? Overweight? Could she have had a chest infection?

John shuffled his notes. Yes, she had a fast pulse occasionally and she smoked a few cigarettes a week. She was mildly obese. And she wheezed on exercise. But none of that, he added, was unusual for her age.

I gave evidence next. 'Dr Adam, did you find any signs of coronary artery disease?'

'Yes sir. It was mild and proportionate to her age.' The coroner already knew that because it was in my report.

'Did you find evidence of infection in her lungs?'

'No, but there was a slight increase in the secretions. She might have had a cold.'

A newspaper reporter burst into the courtroom, breathless from running, to find the coroner summing up. He warned the court sombrely about the miasma of the Fens and seasonal chest infections. He emphasised the deceased's poor state of health and concluded that her heart disease made her vulnerable to an infection which lowered her oxygen level. He recorded the cause of her death as 'acute heart failure caused by oxygen deprivation.'

It was a masterly evasion, accurate so far as it went but miles from the truth. John Dupere and I were left speechless. When the court broke up, he was still grasping the plastic bag. 'What do I do with this?' he asked helplessly. 'Get rid of it, you silly beggar,' I hissed. We later heard a rumour that the dead woman was a friend of the coroner's wife. A suicide verdict was never likely.

* * *

During these years when I was learning my trade as a pathologist, I gave little thought to its effects on our children. Jacqui and I tried to protect them from the details of what I did. In consequence they grew up knowing only that Daddy was a doctor who dealt with dead people and often came home smelling of chemicals. As RAF brats they also came to accept the frequent moves that the Service imposed on us. From the age of eight to thirteen, Kate commenced every September term at a different school. Rob was sent off to boarding school to give him some stability in the years before O-levels. That proved particularly important while we were overseas.

My unconventional job meant there was a sense of normality about death in our family. Later, when we lived in a Somerset village, we had a septic tank that was far from efficient. From time to time I would chuck in a dead pheasant or rabbit to encourage decomposition. No child protested. When our pets died, they were usually buried in the garden. It was known that Daddy kept a skeleton called Betty in a cupboard, but that was normal for doctors, wasn't it?

Many years later Lizby wrote, 'We learned there was always a consequence to our actions. Sometimes it was wrapped up in humour, but always with an element of protectiveness. "Don't stick your head out of the train window" and "Don't put a knife in the dishwasher with the sharp end upwards." At some point in Daddy's work life, a disaster had happened. His parenting was filtered through the lens of being a pathologist.'

More than once when Jacqui organized a children's birthday party, I entertained the company with a game called Inquest which I found in a book of party games and for which I take no credit. It was so politically incorrect that I might be prosecuted today. We turned out the lights, lit candles and played haunting music on the stereo. The young guests were blindfolded and had to guess body parts; I handed round skinned grapes for eyes, peanuts for teeth, a wig for hair and a rubber glove filled with iced water. The highlight was an orange into which they were invited to press a finger. It represented an eye socket. The children were in no way overawed. They shrieked with delight and begged for more.

* * *

House prices in the Fens were low and we bought a large Georgian town house in the centre of Chatteris. It had ceilings that were fifteen feet high and a billiards room so large that we called it the ballroom. It was a wonderful home in summer, but not in winter. The sash windows were ill-fitting and rattled in the wind. Once upon a time servants had tended a dozen coal fires; we now struggled to heat one room.

During the first winter we huddled around the fireplace and the children wore gloves in bed to prevent chilblains. There was a coke boiler in the kitchen which warmed nothing but itself. The attic had no insulation. It was as capacious as a cathedral and it generated draughts in which you could fly a kite.

What was to be done? I mentioned earlier, that pathologists are by nature practical people. They are as happy as pigs in clover when digging drains, rewiring houses and restoring old cars. Central heating? No problem. I would show my skills.

I used a specialist firm to design an oil-fired system and ordered everything I needed from a wholesale company. I booked two weeks of annual leave, during which Jacqui took the children to her parental home and gave me the run of the house. I worked from dawn to dusk, pausing only to eat, sleep and consult a local plumber when I ran into trouble. That was fairly often.

Hacksawing through iron pipes, drilling walls two feet thick and laying long runs of copper pipe was mesmerizing as well as hard work. After a time I fell into a reverie. I was once more a dresser on the firm of Mr Turner-Warwick, the Middlesex Hospital's genito-urinary surgeon. When levering up a floorboard and reaching into the void, I imagined that I was delving into a human pelvis. When soldering a joint, I did it as meticulously as if it were a damaged ureter. At night I had dreams about instruments left in operation sites; by day I was neurotic about counting my spanners and wrenches.

No tools went missing, but our cat Zippy had a narrow escape. She was a formidable mouser and always on the hunt. One day she slipped beneath the boards when my back was turned, and I nailed her in. It was two days before I heard her scratching.

The work took far longer than two weeks and lasted until the first frosts arrived. I still had to find a way to lift a 600-gallon oil tank up four feet and onto its base without hiring a crane. The solution was to get some friends around. They were invited to a 'tank up' involving a few beers, and once they arrived they could hardly refuse to help.

With the boiler fired up, the atmosphere in the house changed miraculously. The children shed their gloves, the guinea pigs came out of hibernation and Jacqui sang my praises. But there was a complication. A pebble had found its way into a pipe when it lay on the gravel drive. It clattered round the house and drove us mad until I finally tracked it down with my stethoscope. I disconnected that segment and extracted it. In medical terms it was an embolus.

* * *

At the hospital my casualty duties kept me in touch with clinical medicine. An elderly farmer suffered a heart attack, and I admitted him because the physicians were busy elsewhere. A few hours later the crash alarm sounded, and I led the team which tried unsuccessfully to resuscitate him. A day later I performed his post-mortem and confirmed my own diagnosis. You could call that holistic medicine, but not of the usual kind.

I remember three cases from this period which concerned x-rays and foreign bodies. One was a tenant farmer who was brought to the mortuary in dungarees and full-length rubber boots. They looked nearly new and the soles were impressively thick. His clothes were soaked with water. He had been hosing down equipment in a yard and no one had witnessed his death.

There was a contact burn on one hand, but no earthing point and his thick boots should have insulated and protected him. But I was sure that he had electrocuted himself, probably by hosing water onto a live source. The puzzle remained until I sent the boots to be x-rayed. They were of foreign make and the soles were reinforced with enough steel plates and tacks and screws to hang a door.

On another occasion I was on casualty duty when a young builder's mate presented with a swollen knee and two days of pain. He was evasive about the history and denied any injury. He only wanted to get pain killers and leave. I ordered an x-ray. A nail lay within the joint space, slightly bent. Confronted with the evidence, the man admitted using a pneumatic nail gun of which he had no training. He was afraid of losing his job. When I told him without exaggeration that he might have lost his leg, he burst into tears.

The third case created much amusement in the doctors' mess. The Ely police brought in a teenage girl who was found beside the road in Littleport. She was examined by Nick Mumford, the junior surgeon and my former Middlesex colleague. He told me, 'She had a mass of scars on her abdomen from surgical operations and no plausible explanation for them. I was pretty sure she was a Munchausen, so I ordered an abdominal x-ray.'

Munchausen syndrome is a psychological disorder named after an 18th century German baron who travelled widely and told unbelievable tales about his adventures. To attract attention, Munchausen patients pretend to be ill; they deliberately fake symptoms like abdominal pain, fits and migraines. Believe it or not, they swallow foreign bodies in order to get themselves cut open.

Bingo! Nick was right. The x-ray showed a three-inch nail lying within the girl's stomach.

He continued the story. 'I put up a drip and prepped her for surgery next morning. The night nurse, bless her, pinned a plastic label to the bottom of her bed which said, 'Nil by mouth.' She secured it with a safety pin. When the porter came to bring her to theatre, neither the pin nor the label could be found. You can guess where we found them. In my view, the term safety pin is a misnomer.'

* * *

My final story from this period involves a foray into general practice. Dr P., an elderly single-handed GP in a village close to Chatteris, asked me to do some surgeries. I liked the idea, but I hesitated. It would keep my clinical skills fresh, and I needed the money, but moonlighting was not approved by the RAF and my prescribing was rusty. My great friend Trevor Betteridge was a senior RAF histopathologist and he regularly moonlighted. He told me there was nothing to it.

'Only doctors fresh out of training use a lot of different drugs. I have three prescriptions. Tetracycline for infections, steroid ointment for skin and Valium for mental problems. One of them always does the trick.'

His nonchalance reminded me of Dr William Osler's maxim that the young physician starts life with twenty drugs for each disease, and the veteran physician has one drug for twenty diseases.

Dr P. put up his brass plate in the 1930s, when leeches and cupping were still used. I knew that he practised from home, but I was surprised to find what that meant. At the bottom of his garden there was a wooden shed, not much larger than a single garage. Into it were crammed a waiting room, a consulting room, a toilet and a dispensary. (The latter was more of a cupboard.) The consulting room had a bunk and equipment for sterilizing instruments, aspirating cysts, cauterizing the uterine cervix, lancing abscesses, examining the eye and the rectum, and a lot else.

There was no receptionist, nurse or dispenser. Dr P. ran the entire operation by himself. He showed me how to unlock the shed and to note the order in which the patients were queuing, for he had no appointment system.

'No time for that sort of thing. First come, first served. And always write a prescription if you're asked. Fen folk expect to take a bottle of medicine home. They feel cheated if they don't get one.'

He dispensed his potions from the cupboard, labelling the bottles by hand and keeping a record of what was used. This made consultations exceedingly drawn out. If he wanted to examine a lady's breast or private parts, the next female patient was asked to act as a chaperone. If none was available, the examination was postponed.

After I proved myself, he invited me to take surgeries on Saturday mornings. 'That's an unusual time for a surgery,' I remarked. 'Do you get many patients?'

'Oh yes. During the war they were soldiers on 48-hour passes. They'd get a dose of the clap and decide not to see their MO. They'd turn up here for a shot of penicillin and tell their girl friends they'd seen me for back ache.'

'But ... I don't get it. The war was over years ago.'

'Of course, but the long-distance lorry drivers find it convenient.'

In spite of the primitive arrangements, I enjoyed my GP sessions. I imagined myself walking in the footsteps of my grandfather who doctored in Yorkshire in the early 1900s. He dripped chloroform onto an open mask with one hand and whipped out tonsils on the kitchen table with the other.

Unfortunately things did not end well. The doctor's wife died suddenly, and the loss hit him hard. His daughter phoned me in the middle of the night after the funeral. Her father was out of his wits, roaming the house with a spade and bawling that he could not live without her. Would I come immediately?

It was unclear whether he intended to disinter his wife or to dig a hole and lie alongside her. I hurried over and gave the poor fellow intravenous Valium. But I could do nothing to save his practice, which collapsed soon afterwards.

* * *

The years in the Fens passed quickly and pleasantly. At the RAF hospital I had one foot in the lab and one on the wards. At home I studied for my exams surrounded by a rumbustious young family and a lively circle of friends. I was consumed with the present and gave little thought to the future. But the day was approaching when my RAF commission would end and there would be decisions to make.

16

Setting a New Course

In 1975 I re-enlisted for eight more years and was happy to do so. It came about in a curious way. An elderly woman in Ely developed a severe blood loss anaemia which baffled my colleagues. The poor soul was x-rayed, scanned, examined under anaesthetic, and subjected to every form of endoscopy. All their efforts were in vain. She died undiagnosed on the ward and came to my attention.

A pathologist is sometimes described as a doctor who can give all the answers 24 hours after the patient has died. And so it proved in this case. At post-mortem I discovered a rare stomach growth which started life as a benign tumour and after many years had turned malignant. Somehow it had managed to evade detection. I was intrigued at the behaviour of the tumour and made a study of it and similar tumours. Later I presented my findings to a professional meeting at RAF Halton.

It went down well. Demonstrations before an audience of pathologists in which the pathologist outshines the clinicians generally do, and I was definitely the hero of my own tale. Later that day Air Vice-Marshal Roger Mortimer, who was my ultimate boss, summoned me to his office. His opening question took me by surprise.

'Adam, how would you like to specialise in tissue diagnosis? We'll send you to the Hammersmith for training and you'll be posted to Washington DC to complete it. Accompanied by your family, of course.'

That was an offer, spiced with bribery, to take up histopathology, which you may recall is the diagnosis of diseases at a cellular level using a light microscope. I had not previously considered histopathology as an option and took the offer home to discuss with Jacqui. It was a big step and would mean a huge upheaval of our family plans and our children's education. Intellectually it appealed to the scientific side of my schizoid nature. But was I suited to the task?

To do well in tissue diagnosis you need certain attributes. First is the ability to concentrate intensely for lengthy periods, so you need patience and stamina. You must stare unblinkingly down a microscope, shutting out background noises and wandering thoughts. You need a sharp eye for detail and a keen visual memory. You must simplify complex findings for colleagues who may be less scientifically minded, so you need good communication skills. And you won't get far if you are colour blind.

How does one learn the trade? The answer lies in the riddle, 'How can you tell when a stick is crooked?' It is to lay a straight stick alongside it. You learn histopathology by studying countless slides of normal muscle, nerve, fat, gut, skin, bone and so on. You are like the trainee bank clerk who scrutinizes countless genuine bank notes to be able to tell a counterfeit one at a glance.

Then you proceed to study an even greater number of slides of diseases in their various forms. You learn the subtle changes in the structures of tissues and in the size, shape, colouring and density of cells. You constantly compare the slides under your microscope with the pictures in your memory bank.

At the same time you must learn about the diseases themselves from textbooks and learned journals, and you do so in far greater depth than you did as a medical student. You study, study, study! Everything is grist to the mill: infections, inflammations, parasites, poisoning, benign tumours, malignant tumours, blood disorders, biochemical disorders, immune disorders, degenerative diseases, trauma and any other affliction you can think of. You master their origins, their features, their natural course, their effects and their response to treatment.

Now let me describe the basic technology, without boring you to death (if I can). It has changed little since it was introduced in the 1840s. It involves embedding tissue samples (biopsies) in paraffin wax, shaving off ultra-thin slices with a wickedly sharp blade called a microtome, fixing them on glass slides and staining the slides different colours with chemical reagents. That is a considerable simplification and omits many modern developments, but it will suffice.

The pathologist's role starts with measuring and photographing the specimen and dictating a description. It may be a bulky organ like a stomach or a breast, or a small one like uterine curettings or a morsel of skin. If it is bulky, he carefully selects samples from it. If small, he orientates it to obtain the most information.

After the technicians have made the slides, he studies them under a light microscope. In complex cases there may be fifty or more of them. He makes his diagnosis and dictates a report. Everything has to be done with extreme care, for there are infinite opportunities for making mistakes, by muddling specimens in the operating theatre, by transposing them at the cut-up table, by poor orientation, by mislabelling the slides, or by a clerical error in the typed report. The process has built-in safeguards, but none are wholly foolproof.

The uniqueness of the specialty lies in the histopathology report. Other laboratory reports are numbers generated by machines and require interpreting. It is in effect a letter from one consultant to another and is his professional opinion. It carries his signature, and he stakes his reputation on it. A wrong diagnosis can have devastating consequences for the patient so he must be clear and concise. Surgeons detest ambiguities.

I knew of an apocryphal tale that illustrated the point. A hospital advertised in the medical press for a histopathologist, stating that preference would be given to a one-armed applicant. When someone asked why this was, he was told, 'We got fed up with the last chap. He always said, "On the one hand it might be this, and on the other it might be that."'

On the downside I knew from my introductory training that histopathology is a somewhat solitary business. In arriving at a diagnosis you take into account the clinical history, the operative findings and information from other sources like radiology, haematology, serology, biochemistry and immunology. Putting all that information together and processing it with the microscope findings is time consuming. You make a lot of phone calls, and you share cases with your colleagues (if you have any) but nobody pretends that histopathology is sociable.

'Wouldn't you miss patients and ward rounds? Jacqui asked. 'It sounds as if you'd spend all your time with your microscope and a dictating machine. Wouldn't it get boring?'

She had a good point, but I knew that histopathology is full of surprises and it is difficult to be bored in the presence of infinite variety. And I knew that there were moments of high drama. Imagine for a moment the situation of a surgeon who is halfway through an operation when he encounters an unexpected growth. The operation is halted. Is it malignant or benign? Should he disregard it or remove it? If malignant, do the malignant cells extend into the blood vessels and lymphatic channels? How widely should he cut?

To answer these questions, he requests a frozen section. A small sample of the growth is hurried to the lab and a technician places it in a cryostat, a machine which rapidly freezes and preserves the tissue. He cuts ultra-thin slices and stains them by hand. The procedure takes only a few minutes. The technicians vie with each other to knock seconds off the laboratory record.

Meanwhile the operating theatre is Sleeping Beauty's palace. The patient slumbers under drapes thrown over the operation site. The surgeon waits impatiently, the anaesthetist fiddles with his dials and the theatre sister hovers by the phone. Time stands still. Everything waits upon Prince Charming.

In his office the pathologist struggles, poor fellow. Frozen section slides are never as good as paraffin-embedded ones. Ice crystals tear and crinkle the tissue and the dyes do not take as well. Nonetheless he must do his best, if only to give a provisional answer and hope that the paraffin sections will confirm it.

In the end, after considering all the pros and cons at length, I accepted the air vice-marshal's offer of further training and two years in America. Soon I was posted back to RAF Halton. I became a 'bean stealer,' a married officer who enjoyed subsidized food and lodging intended primarily for single officers, and who returned home at weekends.

Halton House, the officers' mess in question, was known as the Gilded Cage for reasons which will become clear later. It was administered separately from the messes of the nursing sisters. There were two of them, known as Tampax Towers for the junior sisters and Menopause Mansion for the seniors.

During the week I attended a course in advanced histopathology at the Royal Postgraduate Hospital in Hammersmith. It was hard work because medical science was changing at a breath-taking rate. Let me quote Dr William Osler again. (You can tell that he's one of my heroes.) Over 100 years ago he told his students, 'Gentlemen, half of what we have taught you is in error and furthermore we do not know which half it is.'

* * *

Back in the Cambridgeshire Fens our house took a long time to sell. My mother, who lived in Tenerife, was staying with us and by great misfortune she underwent the kind of ordeal which fate reserves for medical families. She was investigated at RAF Hospital Ely for abdominal pains. During an exploratory operation the surgeon excised an object the size of a cashew nut, thinking it was a lymph node.

It was a disastrous error because he amputated the tip of a diverticulum. A diverticulum is an out-pouching of the bowel like a small balloon. It fully deserves its Latin name which literally means 'a wayside inn of ill repute.' All manner of complications follow if it develops an infection or a leak. Peritonitis set in and by the time it was recognized Mother was in kidney failure. The RAF scrambled a helicopter to evacuate her to its renal dialysis unit at Halton.

At one point it seemed she would die. She underwent a second operation to drain a pelvic abscess and developed a fistula. When she came back to us two months later, she needed a great deal of love and care. Jacqui had the job of nursing her and she coped wonderfully well. Dealing with a faecal fistula is tough enough if you are a trained nurse and Jacqui was not one. And my mother was a plaintive patient, understandably so.

The end of that story was a farce. Group Captain Covell was still the commanding officer at RAF Ely, and he asked me to call in. He had a sheepish expression. 'Andy, I've had a signal from the Min of Def about your mother. Bit of a surprise, really.'

'What's that sir?'

'They've ruled that for medical purposes she's an unentitled dependent.'

'So what?'

'It seems you owe them £3,000 for the helicopter.'

I was speechless. The RAF nearly bumped Mum off and it was sticking the bill on me!

The CO added, 'I'm sorry about this, Andy. They want to know how you'll pay.'

'I've a better idea. Why don't they file their bill alongside my mother's diverticulum?'

'I don't follow you.'

'Right up the rectum. I won't pay a penny.'

The RAF could court martial me or the Ministry of Defence could bring a civil suit. Either way I'd see them in court. I heard no more of the matter.

The house sale finally went through, and we moved into married quarters at RAF Halton in preparation for the greater move to America. The house backed onto the Chiltern Hills and had fine views over the Vale of Aylesbury. After the flatness of the Fens the children loved it, especially Kate who had an adventurous spirit and often disappeared for long dog walks in the beech woods.

In 1976 Britain experienced its hottest summer in living memory. Day after day the temperature reached 32°C somewhere in England, and the South-West was without rain for many weeks. The government passed a Drought Act and farmers shipped their cattle north as the grass withered and died. In the RAF we wore tropical uniform and worked tropical hours. The idea of climate change had not taken root and you loved or hated that summer according to your constitution.

In July we took a holiday 650 miles away on Benbecula in the Outer Hebrides, a place so remote that my father referred to it as *Ultima Thule*. The white sands, blue skies and blistering heat made it seem like the Caribbean. We lodged with an 85-year-old widow whose first language was Gaelic and who told us about the days when the islands were self-sufficient in all but tea and coffee.

We dug for mussels, fished for cod, and combed the beaches for cuttlefish shells. One day Rob and I climbed Ben Mhor, the highest peak in the Hebridean chain. Below us the islands and the Minches which separate them from the mainland looked like a fairy's map.

It baffles me that British families return year after year to crowded European resorts, leaving their children ignorant of the treasures that lie within the British Isles. The reason usually given is the weather. That does not count with me. You do not go to Scotland for the weather; you go there for Scotland. The same applies to Ireland and Wales.

Back home I had bought a shotgun from a catering officer who was disenchanted with shooting after he carelessly blew the side of his boot away. Fortunately the wound was slight.

I joined the Halton shooting syndicate, an eclectic mixture of officers and farmers. The company was good, but the bags were small. We invested in 300 poults each year but got few of them back for the pot. The locality was built-up and our coverts were poached. We spent a lot of time erecting pens, clearing undergrowth and patrolling against poachers.

On New Year's Day 1977 we bagged fourteen brace of pheasants, which was a record. One man downed a bird that sailed into the settling pit of the station's sewage farm. His dog promptly went after it, and when it emerged with the corpse in its jaws the pong was indescribable. The officer in charge of the shoot ordered the owner, the dog and the bird home without delay.

An indescribable pong

Soon after that I had an abdominal x-ray for minor symptoms. 'Andy, I see you are a sporting man,' said the RAF radiologist, pointing to a collection of spherules in my appendix region. They were the lead shot which I ingested with Jacqui's excellent pheasant casseroles, and which had lodged there harmlessly ever since. Like many of life's oddities, they would pass in time.

In the spring of that year I passed the primary part of MRCPath (Membership of the Royal College of Pathologists) and was promoted to squadron leader. The road to America was clear. In the remaining time we tried to buy a house around Halton, but everything was hideously costly after Cambridgeshire. In the end we accepted our bank manager's advice that prices had stabilized and would rise no higher. If we put our money in Treasury stock, he said, it would be safe for two years and we might even save a bit. It was the worst financial advice I ever received.

Overseas postings are far more disruptive than domestic ones. You would have thought that we were leaving the country for ever. Our fridge-freezer, washing machine, and two cars went under the hammer. Our pets were entrusted to family members and our furniture to a storage firm. Both grandmothers promised to keep a watchful eye on Rob, who was 13 and about to become a boarder at Stowe School, not far from Halton. But first he accompanied us to America for the last month of the summer holidays and we were delighted at that.

In August 1977 the five of us climbed aboard a Transport Command VC10 at RAF Brize Norton and flew off on the next adventure.

17

Ay Eff Eye Pee

It was not a good time to arrive in the USA. The heat of Washington DC was sweltering, and the public mood was one of despair. The headlines read, 'The king is dead!' Elvis Presley had died just days before, leaving millions of worshippers numb with grief.

The hotel that was booked in advance turned out to be the kind that did not insist on the guests having luggage. I took one look at its seedy interior and herded the family back into the taxi. At the far superior spa hotel where we settled, Jacqui immediately slipped a disc hefting a suitcase onto a bed.

In the first week we rented a house, bought a car, found schools for our girls and tried to master the geography. The British Embassy advised us where it was safe and not safe to live, and Rockville in Maryland seemed as good as anywhere. The house was in a street which was bright with hibiscus, oleanders and bougainvillea. The rent was reasonable, probably because the son of the owners had died by suicide in the basement. I assured them that it did not deter me, and made a note not to tell Jacqui.

The US Armed Forces Institute of Pathology (AFIP) was on the campus of the Walter Reed Army Medical Centre. I had heard a lot about it, but nothing prepared me for a mammoth fortress with no windows, and concrete walls eight feet thick. It rose through six storeys and occupied as much space beneath the ground as above it.

I reported to the director, Captain Elgin Cowart of the US Navy. He was a rangy southerner who gripped my hand in a vice and welcomed me to what he described as the largest, most specialised and costliest pathology laboratory in the world. It employed 700 staff, including more than 100 pathologists and scientists.

'Some guys find it claustrophobic but if you've served on a nuclear sub, you'll love it.' (I hadn't). 'The walls are atomic bomb proof and if – God forbid! – the Russians start anything, it'll be Washington's defence headquarters.'

Working there was surreal. No windows, daylight, or fresh air: just neon strips buzzing like hornets, and air conditioning so bracing you could almost see your breath. In winter we arrived early and left after dark, so we rarely saw daylight. After peering down a microscope for hours, I had an irresistible urge to dash outside and check that the world had not gone up in a mushroom cloud.

The Institute enjoyed the reverence which Americans attach to anything over 75 years old. I first noticed it when Jacqui let slip that her family home, a mill house in the Cotswolds, dated from 1492. A hush fell on the company, as if they were in the presence of Columbus himself.

* * *

AFIP's origins lay in the American Civil War when few doctors had experience of modern warfare. Poor hygiene, poor surgery, gangrene and camp fever took a fearful toll on the wounded. The Unionist command was so concerned that in 1862 it directed its medical officers to collect 'all specimens of morbid anatomy, surgical or medical, which may be regarded as valuable, together with projectiles and foreign bodies removed.' These grisly objects were to be forwarded to the office of the Surgeon General in Washington DC, so they could be examined in the army's military museum.

The thinking behind the order was ahead of its time: to establish a reference point, to discover what was going wrong, and to introduce sound surgical practice and quality control.

The specimens were mostly amputated limbs which were pickled in brandy, packed into barrels, and shipped by rail to Washington. It did not take long for the railroad workers to discover what they were missing, which was literally gut-rot liquor. They fell to drilling the barrels. The condition of both the specimens and the workers deteriorated until armed guards were posted on the wagons.

Deteriorating conditions among the railroad workers

One of the original specimens was on display in the AFIP museum. It came from General Daniel Sickles, who lost a leg on the first day of the battle of Gettysburg in 1863. A glass case contained the shattered bone, together with the cannon ball that struck it. An ink drawing showed the general inspecting them. He was said to visit his leg every year on the anniversary of the battle.

In time the army military museum became AFIP, a centre for teaching, research and providing second opinions on problem cases. The big names employed there had Olympian reputations and their diagnoses were rarely disputed. And the service came free, which was a unique thing in American medicine.

Civilian cases outnumbered military ones and the contributors were a mixed bunch. Most worked in hospitals in North America, but some were in bush hospitals so far from civilization that we used a radio ham to send our reports.

There were doctors living behind the Iron Curtain who risked their freedom and perhaps their lives in sending cases to a military unit in the USA. There were others in South American towns with no access to modern lab facilities.

AFIP was devoted to the principle of vertical specialization. A colleague explained it to me in these terms: 'Everything is divided on anatomic lines. We've got a department for diseases of the skin, another for the liver, another for soft tissues, another for infectious, one for parasitic diseases and so on.'

'What happens when two departments have an interest in the same case?' I asked.

'It's a doggone tug o' war. For example, there's one department for the left breast and one for the right. And between 'em there's a guy trying to hive off the nipples.'

The joke was in doubtful taste, but there was a serious thought behind it. Vertical specialization in medicine brings increasing expertise in ever narrowing fields. Someone put it like this: 'You get to know more and more about less and less, until you know everything about diddly-squat.'

The scale of AFIP's operation was astonishing. It had nearly three million pathology cases on file. That amounted to thirty million blocks of tissue embedded in paraffin and a fire hazard that nobody liked to mention. There were fifty million glass slides which weighed over 3,000 tons. I realized why all the reinforced concrete was necessary.

Some pathology cases were vanishingly rare. Staffers boasted that no matter how rare a disease might be, AFIP had a dozen examples on file. Others boasted of having cases of conditions not yet described.

The elitism bred an atmosphere in which rivalries blazed and reputations rose and fell. The department chiefs defended their territories as a lioness defends her cubs and everybody strove to justify their positions by writing scientific papers. If the institute had an unofficial motto it was *Publish or Perish*.

The strangest thing about working there was the absence of contact with surgeons and physicians, not to mention contact with patients. It was medicine in a vacuum, and it ran counter to all that I had been taught. They called it mail order pathology, a fair description except that no money changed hands.

In this intellectual hothouse I came of age professionally. Previously my work had been over-supervised. Now I was a member of a team of experienced practitioners. In the mornings we sat at a multi-headed microscope, taking it in turns to present the cases with our diagnoses. The cases were thrown open to discussion. The department chairman or his deputy steered the meeting, and they were not slow to correct and teach. The sign-out carried the chief's name, so everything was meticulously checked. It was a great learning experience.

After the case conference we telephoned the urgent diagnoses and wrote our reports. (E-mails and text messages lay in the future.) The phone calls often took place across many time zones and caught the contributors at odd hours. Most Americans claim to love an English accent, but for some reason they had difficulties in understanding mine, which I would describe as BBC World Service rather than upper crust.

'Good morning, Dr Hartmann, this is Squadron Leader Adam in the Department of Pulmonary and Mediastinal Pathology at the Armed Forces Institute of Pathology.'

'Hey! Speak slower, feller. I cain't understand you.'

Occasionally the recipient just hung up, thus confirming George Bernard Shaw's view that England and America were two countries separated by a common language.

I appealed to my colleagues for help. They found the situation hilarious and agreed to coach me in a new voice. I practised James Cagney in front of a mirror, drawling 'you-dirty-yellow-bellied-rat' from the corner of my mouth. It worked. The subsequent telephone exchanges went far better.

'Hi! This is Ducter Adam callin' yuh from pulmon-airy and meaty-ass'n-all at Ay Eff Eye Pee in Dee Cee.'

'Sure doc, yuh got an answer for me on that lymph node?'

Sometimes it was my vocabulary not my accent that caused a problem. Before each conference we wrote out a histological description of our cases. I wrote mine in pencil and on one occasion needed to correct it. I turned to my colleague on the next desk. 'Rusty, can you lend me a rubber, please?'

Several faces looked up. Rusty said, 'You've gotta be kidding! What d'ya want a rubber for?'

'I've made a mistake.'

'It's a bit late now, dude!' There were hoots all round. I should, of course, have asked for an eraser.

When you work inside a pressure cooker, you make the most of the time you have outside it. As a family we travelled from the Florida to Ontario and from the outer banks of North Carolina to San Francisco. We made many wonderful trips to go crabbing in Chesapeake Bay, and whitewater rafting in the Blue Ridge Mountains. The children adored the car I bought. It was a Ford Country Squire station wagon which was 21 feet long and had eight seats, a bi-axial tailgate, and every conceivable gadget for its day. Its four-litre engine was insatiably thirsty. When it idled, you could hear the gasoline surging through the carburettors.

My official sponsor and close friend at AFIP was Ken Mueller, a US Air Force colonel from Wisconsin. He started in paediatrics before turning to pathology and at that time was specializing in forensics. He was a Harvard man, a deep thinker, and he owned a ludicrously large library. When I asked if he had read it all, he replied, 'If a man has read the whole of his library, his library is not large enough.'

Ken had done a tour of duty at RAF Halton, so we were able to share history and reminiscences. He had also travelled widely in Europe with his wife Carol. Surveys have shown that more than half of American citizens do not own a passport and one in six never venture beyond their home state. That makes their world view understandably insular; I once had to explain to a bunch of students that the Queen did not have the power of capital punishment. Ken was different and I learned much about America through his eyes, and indeed about my own country. He died ten years ago, and I still miss him.

The years in America were a privileged time. I was attached to British Defence Staff, which meant that Jacqui and I were on the fringe of Washington's diplomatic circle. We met fascinating people of many nationalities and attended some wonderful parties and receptions. One night in May 1979, we were at a cocktail party in the British Embassy to mark the general election. There was uproar as Margaret Thatcher and the Conservatives toppled the Labour government of James Callaghan.

The British ambassador was Peter Jay, Callaghan's son-in-law. His appointment had been controversial on several levels: he was not a diplomat, he had never held public office, his background was in television journalism, and he was just forty years old. As the polling results came in over a live link, the ambassador's face turned to thunder while many of the British guests could barely contain their glee. Jay did not survive the change of regime and returned to television.

In November 1978 a disaster took place which shook even the most hardened of my colleagues. It was a massacre that killed more Americans in peacetime than any crime before the destruction of the Twin Towers. It is a historical footnote that they would rather forget.

Its perpetrator was a white religious leader from California called Jim Jones. He created a movement which had the classic features of a cult: a charismatic leader who claimed divine powers; manipulation and deceit; bogus healings; sexual abuses; rigid control over its members' lives; and blackmail and violence towards those who tried to escape.

At the height of its popularity the Peoples Temple in San Francisco had thousands of members, most of them poor black families who handed over their social security benefits to the cult. When the Temple attracted opposition, Jones induced 1,000 of them to migrate to a commune he built in remote jungle in Guyana, South America. He called it Jonestown.

There his megalomania caused the catastrophe. The US Congress became concerned at what it heard, and a congressman called Leo Ryan brought down reporters and photographers on a fact-finding mission. Jones panicked, and at the end of the visit, when the party was on the point of boarding a light airplane, Ryan and four others were shot dead. Jones then induced most of his followers to drink a fruit punch laced with cyanide. Those who refused were forcibly injected with cyanide. In this horrific killing-cum-suicide, 918 people perished. A third of them were children. Jones shot himself in the head, too afraid or cowardly to drink the poison.

The Guyanese government was unable to cope with the disaster and the bodies were flown back in aluminium coffins to Dover Air Force Base in Delaware, a two-hour drive from Washington DC. A team of pathologists from AFIP undertook the gruesome task of identification. The bodies had been lying for days in tropical heat, and many were beyond visual recognition.

I was not on the team and had no wish to be. Memories of the Trident disaster six years earlier came back, and I knew this one would be far worse. Ken Mueller was a lead investigator and performed the post-mortem on Jones, so I learned all the details. Everyone at AFIP got caught up in the horror of the event and the discussions and the presentations that followed. Some of the personnel working at the Dover air base developed post-traumatic stress disorder, and they were not just the doctors but airmen, undertakers and civilian volunteers. The condition was little understood at that time and psychologists believed that it was confined to experiences in war zones. We discovered that it was greater with youth, inexperience, lower rank, and a higher degree of exposure to the carnage. In that respect Jonestown did medicine a favour, by highlighting the syndrome.

The massacre apart, I look back on my two years at AFIP with fondness. It was a crucial period in my career. I learned a great deal of pathology and wrote papers which helped my curriculum vitae. I was appointed a visiting clinical professor at the United States Armed Forces Medical School in Bethesda. That was the lowest rung on the academic ladder, but it looked good on paper. The students were veterans of the war in Vietnam who took a drop in rank to enrol. Their medals, crew cuts and barked responses to my questions reminded me how unmilitary my life was.

* * *

Sadness descended on us in the middle of our time in America. My father, who was in his 70s, was diagnosed with multiple myeloma, a malignant condition of bone marrow cells. It was in an advanced stage, and he presented with jaundice and kidney failure. He was admitted to Torbay General Hospital and his consultant phoned and advised me to return home without delay. The Services are brilliant in these circumstances. The RAF got me a seat on the first available flight to Heathrow and a staff car was waiting there.

When I walked into Dad's hospital room, his jaundiced face lit up and he smiled through his pain. 'That didn't take you long!' He was hoping against the odds that I might know a miraculous treatment that would turn the situation around. But all I could do was examine his blood and bone marrow slides, discuss the treatment with the consultant and assure him that everything possible was being done.

He had started radiotherapy but to little effect. As doctors, we both knew that the treatment would prolong his suffering and only delay his death by a few months. I realized this would be our last meeting. I had nothing to offer him medically and I longed to bring him some inner peace and comfort. But how could I do that? That was a spiritual matter. With all my medical knowledge and familiarity with death, I had nothing to offer.

The next eight months were an awful time for him and for my stepmother Edna, who nursed him single-handedly in their village on Dartmoor. She had no nursing experience and joked, 'I'm better at flower arranging!' but she did a wonderful job. He hung on through fractures, infections, ambulance trips, blood transfusions and weeks of being bedridden during the winter.

At work my chief told me, 'You're always a boy as long as your father is alive.' I knew it and dreaded losing him. I wrote to him two or three times a week. I also knew that forgiveness was an important matter and begged him to forgive my mother for the events of thirty years ago. But he told me that I did not understand. He died early in 1979, leaving a huge void. I felt that I had failed him.

Shortly after our return to the UK, it happened again. A family friend, a man of whom I was extremely fond and who had been extremely good to me, had prostatic cancer and was dying at home. I went to visit him, and this time received an explicit appeal. 'Andy, is there anything you can do to help?' There was nothing. I desperately wanted to bring him comfort but did not know how to begin.

People talk about death-bed conversions as if they are fairly common events. They are not, as most hospice doctors will testify. In our last days, pain and discomfort distract us, drugs dull our minds, and each breath is an effort. Yes, miracles do happen, but it is not a good time to consider something which we have avoided for years.

* * *

Finally, let me return to AFIP and its fate. During the time that I worked there, it provided an excellent service (without cost), in a country where there's no such thing as a free lunch, and most doctors detest the idea of socialized medicine. Its work seemed to me to be so humane and so beneficial that it would carry on indefinitely.

I was wrong. After 2000 the Institute fell victim to cuts in the federal budget, and despite strong opposition it was closed down. A mountain of glass slides, wet tissues and paraffin blocks was carried off in goodness knows how many army trucks. The building was too massive to bulldoze, and a civilian occupant was found.

A similar fate overtook the medical, dental and nursing services of our own Armed Forces. The end of the Cold War in 1991 signalled huge cuts in the defence budget. One by one all our military hospitals were closed down. A small number of specialist doctors and nurses were retained to work in NHS hospitals and to share their facilities.

I am no militarist, but I greatly regret that wholesale destruction. In a stroke the expertise, the loyalty and the *esprit de corps* which had been built carefully up over generations were thrown away. Servicemen and women were deprived of health benefits and comforts which they expected and had long enjoyed. British medicine was deprived of a model, since military hospitals were frequently superior to civilian ones in clinical practice, administration and hygiene.

What is more, the NHS lost an invaluable source of relief. The Armed Forces Covenant of 2010 addressed some of the disadvantages of military life, but it could not bring back what had been destroyed. As I write, the NHS reels from the effects of the Covid pandemic, underfunding, understaffing, strikes and excessive bureaucracy. It could well use the back-up that the Armed Forces were once able to provide.

18

Going in for Trade

Before we left for America, our bank manager in Aylesbury assured us that the housing market was stable. Two years later he huffed and puffed in his chair. He could have not been more wrong. Prices had doubled and were still rising alarmingly when we returned. And he had not thought to contact us while we were away.

'Please believe me, not even the governor of the Bank of England could have foreseen it.' He talked about the London business boom, the broadening of the commuter belt and the housing shortage. Blah-blah-blah.

Then he smiled ingratiatingly. 'The good thing is that I can offer you a really substantial mortgage.' I felt like punching him.

Jacqui and I now faced the predicament of many families. We could not afford a home where we needed to live. We toured the estate agents but declined one brochure after another. Everything was beyond our means.

Then an opportunity appeared under our noses. On the edge of the RAF station lay the Saxon village of Halton, from which it gets its name. It had great charm, and in those days it boasted a post office-cum-shop as well as a village hall, a tennis club and a church. A branch of the Grand Junction canal ran through it. Commercial traffic had long since disappeared, making it a tranquil home for moor hens and kingfishers.

The post office was also the village stores and an off-licence. The accommodation included four bedrooms. The elderly spinsters who had run it for years were selling up and the place would suit us royally. But they wanted a high price which we could only afford if we continued to run the business. That meant a commercial mortgage at 16% interest.

All in all, it was a gamble and I am not a gambling man. The shop did not make a big profit, the building reeked of damp, and there was an invigorating absence of central heating. The newspapers said the Post Office was in the process of closing many sub-post offices. Did this one have a future?

I took the matter to my new CO, Group Captain Frank Jones, who had succeeded the air vice-marshal. We called him Great Uncle Bulgaria, after the musical director of the Wombles, those funny creatures which inhabit burrows on Wimbledon Common, collect litter and sing catchy tunes. Exactly why we called him that I cannot remember. Perhaps it was because of his gait, which was rolling and unmilitary.

Frank seemed a wise bird and I hoped for good advice, but I received a douche of cold water. 'Sorry Andy, definitely not on. The Service does not approve of its officers going in for trade. Nor do I.' That was all very well for him, I thought. He had a fine house which he bought before prices went haywire.

'Sir, I've checked and it's not forbidden under Queen's Regulations. My wife would be the responsible party. And we have no alternative.'

We argued and neither of us budged. Finally he said, 'If you go ahead with this purchase, it's on your head. If you're spotted in uniform behind a counter, you'll be charged with conduct unbecoming an officer.'

I would have preferred his blessing to a threat, but I was not going to be bullied. Sometimes the biggest risk is to take no risk at all. To friends in America I wrote, 'We are pressing ahead. The British are after all a nation of shopkeepers, and the liquor licence will be a consolation if things do not turn out as we hope.'

So began a strange season, which for me was dominated by my final MRCPath examination and for Jacqui by running a business as well as being a wife and mother. Learning to manage the shop was no easy matter but she inherited a treasure named Florence who knew the ropes. However the Post Office bosses were neither helpful nor benign. Every

Saturday Jacqui had to perform an audit of the week's business, counting every penny and every postage stamp, and if the columns did not match they made her life miserable. Mercifully she missed by two decades the dreadful scandal in which the Post Office wrongly prosecuted over 700 postmasters and postmistresses for alleged false accounting and theft.

Strange noises came from a cellar which had been sealed off for years. When a trapdoor was finally unscrewed, an army of frogs invaded the shop. We dealt with them and with woodworm and rising damp. A firm of builders installed central heating, for I did not care to repeat my plumbing feat at Chatteris.

An invading army

The Post Office also insisted that we convert a storeroom into a miniature Fort Knox with fireproof walls, bullet proof screens and alarms. Exactly one year after that expense, it announced that it was closing the sub-post office permanently.

Jacqui coped wonderfully with these disruptions while selling pork pies and cheese rolls to the RAF apprentices on their lunch break. I helped out in the evenings. After work I would change out of uniform and drive twenty miles to a cash-and-carry warehouse in Luton. I loathe shopping at the best of times and Jacqui's lists were mammoth, but I steeled myself to the task. I drove home with the car packed tightly with catering packs of food and drink. After everything was unloaded and stored, it was time for bed.

The shop taught us both a lively respect for the men and women who run small businesses. They have to live ordered and disciplined lives. Our weekend breaks were few and carefully planned, and our holidays never lasted longer than a week.

In the midst of this activity, I completed a book which I had started to write when I lived in the officers' mess. Halton has a fascinating history. The manor was bought in the mid-1800s by the Rothschilds who were Jewish bankers, and parvenus in Victorian society. They needed land to be accepted by the aristocracy. They fixed their sights on the Vale of Aylesbury, to which access from London by train was easy. By 1900 they had accumulated 30,000 acres and five great country houses.

Alfred Charles de Rothschild was to my mind the star of the show; a millionaire playboy who was a bachelor, an art connoisseur and a collector. He built Halton House as a luxurious weekend retreat to entertain ambassadors, politicians, opera singers and actresses. Besides three dozen domestic staff, sixty gardeners and a twelve-man fire brigade, he had his own string orchestra and a private circus.

We called his chateau the Gilded Cage because of its many gold leaf embellishments, and they gave rise to many gilded stories. For example, that Edward Prince of Wales broke his leg on the back stairs pursuing a maid (untrue, it happened at Waddesdon Manor); that Alfred set up the actress Lily Langtry in a nearby chalet (also untrue); and that chorus girls replaced marble nymphs on plinths in the Italian gardens during stag parties (unlikely).

In more recent years, Halton House has doubled as an opulent filmset location for *The King's Speech*, *Downton Abbey*,

The Crown, and even *Bridgerton*. But at the time, our children loved the house for other reasons. The public rooms were vast and lent themselves to endless hide-and-seek and games of marbles played on carpets the size of tennis courts.

I decided to use my forensic skills to unravel fact from fiction. It was a race against time. The villagers who remembered the Rothschild era were dying off. I advertised widely and used a tape recorder to interview those who responded. I tracked down RAF veterans and gave them tours of their old haunts while plying them with questions.

Alfred flourished at Halton like a sultan for more than three decades. When the Great War broke out Lord Kitchener, a personal friend with whom he lunched every week, was the Secretary of State for War. Kitchener urgently needed training camps and over the lunch table Alfred offered the use of his estate. It was a splendid offer, made on the sole condition that the property was returned in the same condition after the war.

Like many a patriotic gesture, it did not turn out well for the patriot. A senior officer who saw Halton in 1914 wrote, 'There was nothing here except a house and 7,000 pheasants which no doubt the New Army ate ... I did not see it again until 1919. There was nothing here then except workshops and a sea of wooden huts.'

He forgot to mention the parade grounds, rifle ranges, trenches, rubbish tips, roads, railway lines, incinerator units and barbed wire defences. And not least the destruction of Alfred's beautiful beech woods, which were chopped down to provide duckboards for the trenches.

The 3,000-acre estate was ruined. The Government could neither afford to restore it to its previous condition, nor could it give up its investment. It drove a hard bargain and purchased the entire estate for a song. It was then passed to the infant Royal Air Force and Alfred's beloved chateau became the officers' mess.

All these events I chronicled over seven years without a word processor or the internet. The book, titled *Beechwoods and Bayonets*, was published in 1983, shortly before I left the Service.

Meanwhile I sat the final part of the MRCPath exam at Addenbrooke's Hospital in Cambridge. It included a post-mortem examination performed against the clock.

I hoped for a cadaver that had belonged to someone who had been in perfect health until they died suddenly from something obvious like a stroke. Instead I got an elderly man with hospital notes the thickness of a telephone directory. After five days of refrigeration, he was as stiff as a board.

A professor of pathology interrogated me for the longest thirty minutes of my life. Then he told me I had passed, and I drove home in a daze of euphoria. Within a few weeks I passed an Armed Forces' consultant's board and was in charge of the RAF's histopathology department at IPTM. I had reached the pinnacle of my little world.

I was 43 years old, and fully qualified in my specialty; I need never sit another examination. What would I do with the rest of my life? Certainly not let Jacqui run a village shop indefinitely. In the following months I weighed my options.

The RAF had much to offer: good colleagues, pleasant surroundings and job security (but the latter proved illusory). Frank Jones urged me to stay; he believed that officers like me represented an investment that should be repaid. But something was missing. In choosing so narrow a specialty I had painted myself into a corner. A decision to stay in the Service meant working in the same laboratory, and the same office, for 22 more years.

And there was more. My mind was in turmoil. Until then life had revolved around my family, my career and my personal interests. The RAF years were salad days, blissful and relatively carefree, and I look back on them with great affection. But they were also self-centred and shallow. All the time I yearned for something deeper. There had to be more to life.

The 17th century philosopher, Pascal, proposed the idea of a 'God-shaped hole' inside the heart of every man and woman. We vainly try to fill it with the things around us, but the void remains stubbornly empty; only God can fill it. Throughout my life I had filled the hole with things that seemed wholesome: my family, my career, my writing and so on. The time which I spent writing the history of Halton was another example.

I thought of myself as a Christian. After all, I was British and from a white middle-class family. My dad was a doctor and my mother a churchgoer. I attended a public school which held chapel services daily and three times on Sundays. At fourteen I was confirmed by the Bishop of Guildford, and he certainly thought I was a Christian. I *must* be one, surely?

But I had no sense of having a relationship with God, or of being loved by him. We had bibles in the house, but I rarely read one. To me Jesus was a historical figure – a teacher and prophet – from 1900 years ago. He was irrelevant to my world. As for church, we went there at Christmas and Easter, dragging our reluctant children with us. Why did we bother?

At the same time, I was constantly nagged by things in my past. You do not practise medicine for long before you have disasters on your conscience. I had no idea what to do with my guilt and regrets. Repent and seek forgiveness? Not likely! I was a good person, even if I slipped occasionally.

Unable to solve these questions, I shelved them and concentrated on seeing if the grass was greener in Civvy Street. That meant taking locum jobs. Doctors in the Armed Forces were popular as locums because they were a fairly safe bet. Employing a locum is like betting on a horse of unknown performance.

I remember reading about one locum who was an impostor with no medical qualifications. He was careful to impersonate only consultants and he never stayed long in one place. He always chose hospitals where there was plenty of junior staff. On a ward round he would listen to the patient's history, make an examination, and turn to the registrar. 'Hmm, an interesting case. Tell me James, how would you treat the patient?' Then he would ask the SHO the same question, before choosing what seemed the safer course. The scheme worked well until he became over-confident and started prescribing his own treatments. He ended up in prison, having defrauded the NHS of a great deal of money.

I am not disparaging locums, far from it. The overwhelming majority do excellent work and the NHS would collapse without them. And a locum job is a big challenge. You are like a chef assigned to a strange restaurant, employed to prepare a banquet while knowing nothing of the lay-out, the staff or the culinary standard expected. Every detail is new, and every task takes twice the normal time. Nevertheless I enjoyed doing locums and seeing medicine from a civilian perspective. And the NHS hospitals where I worked were agreeably well run.

Around this time I met a lovely man called George Rivas. He was a drug company rep; one of those employees who liaises with hospital doctors and GPs and keep their company's products before their eyes. Back in my Salisbury days the reps bribed us with expensive dinners in fancy restaurants. In Buckinghamshire the hospitality was not so lavish. They tended towards buffet lunches with vol-au-vents and salmon sandwiches, accompanied by free desk diaries.

At a luncheon which George hosted at IPTM I noticed a silver fish in his lapel. In my ignorance I asked him if he were a fisherman. He nodded.

'What do you do, coarse or game fishing?'

He smiled. 'Both. Want to hear about it?'

The stewards were clearing the plates away and the company was filing into the lecture hall. I hung back, listening to George telling me about his Christian faith. I couldn't help warming to his sincerity and plain speaking.

Finally he said, 'Why don't you come to my church, and see what you think?'

I agreed, for politeness' sake. Jacqui did not wish to be involved, so the next Sunday I drove myself to a chapel in Amersham. The pastor was a former veterinary surgeon who gave a stirring sermon unlike any I had heard from a RAF chaplain.

But my enthusiasm did not last. Looking back, I know that the time was not ripe for change, either for my family or for me. I had to be shocked out of my comfortable egocentric life. I had to step into a different world.

19

Musgrove Park Hospital

My RAF commission was going to end in the spring of 1983. By now I was certain that I wanted to obtain a good job outside, settle my family in a permanent home and ensure that our children had continuity of education. Those are the stock reasons for exchanging military life for Civvy Street.

I had no doubts about continuing in histopathology and at this point perhaps I should explain why. People often asked why on earth I chose to work with dead tissues and dead people, often with a sniff as if I should have found something more wholesome.

First and foremost, there is great satisfaction in the work. Histopathologists do not need to be told how important it is. Two-thirds of patients require laboratory investigations to establish a diagnosis and without a diagnosis they cannot be treated safely. This is especially true of cancer patients; it can be disastrous to initiate treatment without a full and accurate histopathology report. And after treatment has started, pathologists monitor the course of the disease.

While pathologists are mainly backroom boys, 'the doctors' doctors,' they also are part of a clinical team. A friendly surgeon will sometimes refer to 'my pathologist,' just as he will refer to 'my anaesthetist.' A pathologist serves his colleagues as well as his colleagues' patients.

Secondly, histopathology is more than the handmaiden of the clinicians; it has a life of its own. There are great opportunities for teaching and research, pushing back the boundaries of knowledge. The work is practical as well as intellectual; it appeals to a practical mind. Histopathologists love to restore old cars, dig drains and mend computers, (and of course install central heating).

Thirdly, the hours are more sociable than in most branches of medicine. If a histopathologist chooses, he can work nine-to-five and never come in at nights or weekends. That keeps him fresh and well-motivated. It is not to say he is socially dysfunctional or lacks empathy with patients. He may simply find illnesses more interesting than the patients who get them. Why should he be blamed for preferring to work with inanimate things?

Fourthly, the absence of patients makes for a quieter and more reflective life. Some doctors say medicine would be the perfect job without them. Most patients are grateful and appreciative, but others are demanding and rude; they raise your blood pressure, give you ulcers and threaten you with lawsuits.

There is a final reason for liking histopathology that is not mentioned in any medical textbook. Human tissues are amazingly beautiful, especially when stained a variety of colours. The essence of histopathology is recognizing variations in the shape, colour and form of cells and structures. Even the abnormal cells have an artistry of their own. You may stare down the microscope and think, 'That's beautiful!' and think again when you remember that they represent a lethal cancer.

All this surprises newcomers to the discipline, just as the beauty of the planets must have surprised Galileo and Kepler when viewed through a primitive telescope. Scoffers refer to histopathology as wallpaper-matching, but histopathologists call it art appreciation.

Consider the human testis. A section through it contains hundreds of tiny closely packed tubules which are filled with the primitive cells that give rise to spermatozoa. Many are caught in the act of mitosis, or cellular division. When you gaze down the microscope, you are looking at a snapshot of the origins of life.

I am surprised that no entrepreneur has thought to print sections of the testis photographically onto table mats or T-shirts. They would make great conversation pieces.

A snapshot of life

* * *

And so it was that one weekend at the beginning of 1983, I drove from Halton in Buckinghamshire to Taunton in Somerset on a fact-finding mission. Its district general hospital was advertising for a consultant histopathologist, and I wanted to scout around before deciding whether to apply.

Musgrove Park Hospital started life in 1941 as the 67th General Hospital of the US Army. Military engineers threw it together in a few months and forty years later it looked as if they had not left. The iconic Oregon pine tree planted in the car park in 1942 had grown to full height. Everything else was frozen in time.

A sprawling collection of single-storey brick buildings were connected by corridors, each designed to be wide enough to fit a Jeep with a stretcher laid across it. I opened an outside door and drew back. 'Quack, quack!' Mrs Puddle-Duck waddled past with her ducklings. The land on which the hospital had been built was marshy, and nobody had given a thought to the local wildlife. She was on the way to her feeding grounds.

My visit was a last-minute decision, and it was quite unofficial. When I rang the bell to the pathology laboratory on a Saturday afternoon, the duty technician might well have refused to admit me. Instead he welcomed me with a grin. 'Spying out the land, eh doc? Good timing – the coast's clear.'

The laboratory resembled a lawyer's office in a Dickens novel, cramped, dingy and dark. All four pathologies shared one big set of rooms, and the sluices and storage cupboards were jammed with equipment. The place was clearly overworked and underfinanced. There was a shortage of automated equipment and computers. The cytology reports were filed in shoeboxes.

The mortuary was a shed with rusting windows and peeling paint. Its walls were one brick thick and had no insulation. My guide informed me, 'The technicians, poor beggars, freeze in winter and bake in summer. In the last flu epidemic they stacked the bodies in the corridor. No room, you see.'

Before I left he gave me a final helping hand. My car's radiator was leaking and he fetched a plastic container and filled it with water. Somebody had written on it the words '24-hour urine collection' with a felt tip pen. I got some strange looks when I topped up the radiator in a pub car park.

Back home I described the situation at Taunton to Jacqui. She said, 'Darling, are you sure it's the right place? It sounds as if it could be awfully hard work!'

That was probably true, but the prospects were attractive. A great deal of money had been allocated for upgrading the hospital, and there would be new pathology laboratories and a new mortuary. Substantial changes were on the way, and I could be part of them. Jacqui and I both wanted to live in the West Country and Taunton seemed a very pleasant spot.

My application went well, and I was appointed to the post. There were less than fifty consultants (today there are over two hundred) and initially I was the only histopathologist. I was responsible for all the surgical pathology, the cytopathology and the post-mortem work.

I was lucky enough to inherit an excellent team of technical staff. A pathologist's success or failure depends on the skill of his technical staff. As the saying goes, you can't make a silk purse out of a sow's ear. At Musgrove Park they were some of the nicest, longest suffering and least appreciated people in the hospital. When I started out they were called lab techs; today they are university graduates and known as MLSOs (Medical Laboratory Scientific Officers). A rose by any other name smells as sweet and they richly deserve their professional recognition.

It turned out that the senior MLSOs were more concerned about my competence than I was of theirs. I was, after all, as an alien out of the RAF. They opened a book and wagered that I would not last more than two months.

Then there were the cytology screeners. Cytopathology is the diagnosis of diseases in cell smears and liquid suspensions as opposed to solid tissues. It is a specialty in its own right, but in my day it was usually overseen by histopathologists. Cytologists perform difficult and demanding work for little reward, mainly examining cervical smears. Their skill lies in distinguishing normal cells from inflammations, infections and pre-malignant and malignant conditions. They are the unsung Cinderellas of the NHS system.

* * *

Life in the NHS proved to be far harder than in the RAF. In Taunton I started out doing the work of two consultants. During the summer of 1983 I faced a wave of road deaths, suicides, cancers and heart attacks. And many of the victims were younger than me, which was depressing.

As a pathologist you know the fragility of life. Death is a heartbeat away. I accepted that, but I struggled with the problem of pain and suffering. Why did terrible things keep happening to innocent people, particularly children? If there was a God who was all-powerful, why did he allow it? I grew angry at a deity of whose existence I was not even convinced. (At this time I had not begun to study near-death experiences.)

There were occasions after the mortuary technicians had left when I slipped into the building, opened the fridge, and gazed on the face of someone I had known. I would wonder, 'Where are you now? Where has all that vitality, wisdom and humour gone? Are you extinguished? Do you live on in another place?' They were the same questions that I asked decades earlier at Heathrow airport.

Of course I never got an answer, apart from the extraordinary sound I heard one evening coming from inside the mortuary fridge. It was half warble and half shriek, and it made my hair stand on end. Occasionally people are certified as dead and revive hours later in an undertaker's parlour. I opened the door and scanned the interior. The noise came from a hearing aid which had detuned and was playing back on itself.

Eerie mortuary sounds

The long hours and the grim harvest began to take their toll. Dylan Thomas wrote: 'Do not go gentle into that good night; old age should burn and rage at close of day. Rage, rage against the dying of the light!' I was not old, but I was raging at the dying of other people's light and at my inability to make sense of life and death.

At the end of 1983 I began to feel ill. The day's work exhausted me; I lost weight and acquired a cough. Then I developed night sweats which really scared me, for they are one of the symptoms of Hodgkin's disease. I had not yet registered with a GP so I stupidly ran lab tests on myself, ignoring Dr William Osler's warning that 'any physician who treats himself has a fool for a patient.' Jacqui would never have tolerated such nonsense but she was back in Buckinghamshire selling our house. I was living in digs in Taunton and deprived of her superior sense.

Between my illness and my folly I was rapidly becoming what the army calls 'unfit for your trade.' So it was almost a relief when, towards the end of a long day, a bacteriologist burst into in my office.

'Andy, we've been running extra tests on specimens which I believe are yours. You've got lung tuberculosis. Pack up your things; you're going into an isolation unit.' I was suspended forthwith.

Exactly how I caught TB was unclear. Its incidence in Britain had dropped dramatically, but in Taunton we diagnosed two or three cases each year in the mortuary. The victims were often reclusive individuals who avoided doctors like the plague. That autumn I had performed a post-mortem examination on a man who had intestinal tuberculosis, which is particularly dangerous to mortuary staff. When the gut is opened, clouds of mycobacteria are released into the air.

However, the chest physician who treated me thought that my infection was probably the result of childhood exposure. It is almost impossible to kill tuberculous microbes totally. They are walled off by fibrous tissue but may be reactivated by conditions like overwork, cancer and steroid treatment.

If the mycobacteria had lain dormant in my lungs for many years, they probably came from my father. That was not a happy thought. What's more, I was the same age as Dad when he contracted the disease. It wrecked his career and he never worked again. Would the same infection and the same microbes wreck mine too?

Back home I received a letter which suggested that might happen. The Somerset Health Authority took a hard line. 'If you are not able to resume your duties within two months, we shall, with regret, have to let you go.' I was new in post and expendable. The RAF would never have treated a man that way. How I regretted leaving its fold!

The pressure increased. By coincidence a doctor with my name (a physicist not a medical man) died and the *British Medical Journal* confused us and published a notice of my death. Friends rang to give their condolences to Jacqui. Not as many as I might have hoped actually, which made me feel worse.

My world was falling apart. I was 44 years old and at night I dreamed of my death.

A feverish brain exaggerates things. My father was poorly treated with the new anti-tuberculosis drugs, and he had to undergo a major operation for a stomach ulcer. All I had to do was heed my doctors, swallow a lot of pills and take things easy. All being well, I would be back at work in a few months. Deep down I knew that, but it did not console me.

The author C.S. Lewis wrote, 'God whispers to us in our pleasures, speaks in our consciences but shouts in our pains. It is his megaphone to rouse a deaf world.' I was in mental pain and not just about my illness. I thought I was a success, but in many ways I was a failure. I thought I was a Christian, but I was a fraud. I had no idea of what I was doing other than pursuing a career, raising my children and putting money in the bank. I had been trained to question everything and to take nothing on trust. My cynicism and arrogance had brought only confusion and unhappiness.

Time went by and things gradually improved. I was declared healthy and returned to work. The arrival of Dr Stephen Smith as a second histopathologist improved the situation immensely. We worked together for sixteen years. Stephen was a wonderful colleague, wise, thoughtful and conscientious. He was better at relationships than me and I learned much from him.

Our home in Buckinghamshire was finally sold, and Jacqui and the children joined me in Somerset. By now my illness had caused me to think deeply about my own mortality: I wanted answers. At a friend's invitation, we started to attend a Baptist church just outside Taunton. For the first time I encountered a faith that was relevant to my problems. The megaphone sounded loud and clear. Every Sunday as we drove home from church, I gripped the wheel and exclaimed to Jacqui, 'That man (the pastor) was speaking to *me*!'

If you are middle-aged and opinionated, the hardest thing about coming to faith is to accept your own helplessness. You cannot earn, argue or bargain your way into heaven. I had to acknowledge that my separation from God (my 'sin') was an insurmountable barrier.

It took me a year to accept that nothing depended on me, and everything depended on what Jesus had done on the cross. Only through accepting him as my saviour could my relationship with God be restored.

By June 1985 I still had many unanswered questions but I was exhausted from arguing, and something had to give. There was no flash of lightning; I simply yielded. I let trust take over, and for the first time in my life I truly encountered Jesus. Jacqui also came to faith in the same week.

Christian faith is not a magic wand that makes your problems disappear. It is a way of life that must be learned. It brings unimagined challenges regarding honesty, forgiveness and loving your neighbour. It also brought Jacqui and me joy, healing, restoration, a new purpose and a new future. It deepened our relationship and love for one another. It revolutionized our lives and does so still to this day.

Many people are sceptical about religious testimonies and this is not a religious treatise, so I'll say no more. My faith has worked wonderfully well for me, and there is no reason that it should not work for others.

* * *

One of the joys of owning a farmhouse in the country was that we had the space to entertain lots of friends. In the summer of 1985 we located as many Middlesex contemporaries as we could and invited everyone to a reunion.

The event was *al fresco*, with most of the company camping in our orchard and the remainder crammed into the house. We played rounders and tag in a field, and barbecued around a campfire. We drank beer under the stars and reminisced about student days. Jacqui had to remonstrate with one prominent GP for relieving himself in the bushes and dowsing a tree peony (no pun intended) which subsequently died.

Apart from that, the reunion was an immense success and started a tradition which has lasted forty years. For reasons that are now forgotten we caused ourselves 'the Slags,' and as we grew more affluent we graduated from tents and holiday-lets to spa hotels with fine restaurants. We do that every summer, and have grown old and fond together.

Let me now return to pathology at Musgrove Park Hospital. I practised there for seventeen years, during which time there were many changes at the hospital and in medicine. Let me give an example which encapsulates those changes.

As a medical student I was often shocked by the size of the pathology specimens which the surgeons submitted for analysis. They were not just gall bladders and appendices; they were entire breasts, stomachs, intestines, kidney and limbs and so on. They filled bucket-sized containers. A year's harvest amounted to a mountain of flesh and a sea of formalin fluid.

Each specimen represented great pain and loss to a patient: the product of cancer surgery performed in old mutilating ways. Some people called it 'heroic surgery.' The phrase irked me; the patients were the heroes, not the surgeons.

At Musgrove Park we kept the big specimens in stainless steel trays when we were working on them. One day a new window cleaner showed up at the laboratory, to clean the inside windows. He managed to ruffle the feathers of Bill

Tripp, our chief MLSO. Bill had been a sergeant in the Royal Army Medical Corps, and you treated him with respect.

The cleaner was on a stepladder polishing away when a specimen pot got in his way.

'Here mate,' he called down, 'Give us a hand, will yuh?'

'Certainly, young man,' said Bill, reaching down to a metal tray. 'Would you like a left hand or a right one?' The cleaner was completely overcome by the offer. Fortunately, he toppled over backwards and not forwards, or the mortuary might have had an extra case that day.

A left or right hand, young man?

Then the wonderful world of endoscopy came along and drastically reduced the number of bulky specimens. Endoscopes are fibre-optic tubes which come in various forms; you can pass one into almost every orifice in the human body. (The umbilicus is an exception, being a *cul de sac*.) Today we have endoscopes for most of the letters of the alphabet: arthroscopes, bronchoscopes, colonoscopes, colposcopes, cystoscopes, gastroscopes, laparoscopes, oesophagoscopes ... down to sigmoidoscopes.

Laparoscopes are used to examine the interior of the abdominal cavity. In the 1980s surgeons learned how to perform keyhole surgery using them; they removed appendices and gall bladders and repaired hernias through very small incisions. The gynaecologists tied off fallopian tubes and performed hysterectomies with them. The genito-urinary surgeons removed prostate glands with them.

My favourite endoscopists were the colonoscopies, who explore up the back passage. Like Captain Kirk of the starship *Enterprise*, their mission was 'to explore strange new worlds; to seek out new life and new civilizations; to boldly go where no man has gone before.'

Colonoscopists love their work. One colleague boasted that it was always a pleasure to look up old friends.

I visited the colonoscopy clinic from time to time to watch the proceedings. The colonoscope is a flexible tube about six feet long packed with high technology gadgets. Its outer surface is shiny black plastic and when resting in its case it resembles a black mamba, coiled and ready to strike. The business end contains an LED light, a video camera, operating forceps, a diathermy loop and a tube which blows air and water into the gut to improve the visibility.

As the operator passes the instrument gently upwards, a view of the interior of the bowel opens up on a screen. It is a similar view to what a London Underground train driver sees, as he passes under the Thames. The route is winding and dark and there are strange noises in the background. These are borborygmi, gurgling sounds made by fluid shifting around the intestines. They are a wonderful example of onomatopoeia.

The experience is not pleasant for the patient, but it is bearable. The instrument weaves from side to side, peeking into every cranny until it reaches something of interest like an ulcer or a polyp. It takes photographs and unsheathes the forceps which remove the lesion or snip a bit off it. This is the precious tissue biopsy on which the pathologist makes a diagnosis. The procedure saves the patient a cutting operation, the surgeon hours of time, and the NHS a great deal of money.

As I mentioned, the colonoscope can improve visibility by inflating and washing a segment of the bowel. At one session the consultant was over-generous with the air. When he removed the instrument the patient, a genteel lady of mature years, emitted a fart which echoed down the corridor. She cried out in distress.

'Oh doctor, was that me?'

'Not at all, Mrs Carter. It's our pathologist Dr Adam. He ate a curry which doesn't agree with him.'

I fled the room.

20

Down Among the Dead Men

I have attempted to demystify the work of a histopathology laboratory and make it sound socially acceptable. That is less easy to do with a mortuary. However bright, well-ventilated and hygienic it may be, it can never be described as a pleasant place. The work is messy, smelly and often nauseating. It is also physically and mentally hard. You have to keep going for hours on end. You do things no other doctors are expected to do, struggling to keep down your breakfast.

The mortuary technicians have it as bad as the doctors, if not worse. They spend their entire day assisting them by opening bodies, removing craniums, sewing up incisions, cleaning up the gore and keeping the tools sharp. They receive and release dead bodies, deal with undertakers and distressed relatives and handle an unending flow of paperwork. Good technicians are worth their weight in gold. They used to be referred to as mortuary attendants. Today they are APTs: anatomic pathology technicians. They have my undiluted admiration.

We had two excellent APTs. The senior man, John Swift, and his wife Josie became good friends of mine. John was very experienced and had the esteemed reputation of being 'the fastest needle in the West.'

As a youth he had played in a Salvation Army band and now played his accordion and keyboard at pubs and festivals. His pride and joy was a motorcycle of dazzling beauty. It was a Honda Gold Wing tourer, complete with a matching trailer. Both were finished in gold paint and so were John's helmet and leathers. On a fine day he arrived at the mortuary like Helios, the Greek sun god, descending in his chariot. Our other technician, Chris Paine, was a Harley Davidson fanatic and the two men argued continually about the merits of their vehicles. Sometimes we had to shut them up.

Some people regard mortuary work as a dead-end job. Others, like three small boys in my first week in Taunton, are intrigued by it. One morning a shadow fell over the porcelain table in the mortuary. I looked up to see heads framed in a skylight. These urchins had clambered onto a low wall that provided cover for the hearses. They grinned at me, waiting for the show to begin.

'Those little blighters again!' exclaimed John Swift. 'I'll give them a taste of blood and guts.' He picked up a mop to chase them off.

That incident demonstrates the ghoulish streak that is dormant in most of us. The philosopher Plato wrote about it in the *Republic*. He tells of an Athenian who is walking outside the city walls when he spots a pile of corpses. They have been left there by the public executioner. He yearns to look at them and is disgusted by his yearning. He dithers and covers his eyes. Finally, desire overcomes him and he rushes up to the bodies, opens his eyes wide and exclaims, 'There you are, curse you! Have a really good look. Isn't it a lovely sight?'

Before going further, let me clear up the difference between an autopsy and a post-mortem examination (or simply 'post-mortem'). The Greek word *autopsein* means to see something with your own eyes. It is what happens at a dissecting table, nothing more.

A post-mortem examination is far more than that. It includes the results of blood and biochemical tests, toxicology, x-rays, photographs and statements from witnesses and scenes of crime officers. An autopsy takes an hour or so to do and involves one person who is called the prosector. A post-mortem investigation may take months or years and involve a whole team.

Autopsies have a history that goes back 5,000 years to ancient Egypt. When a pharaoh died, priests removed his innards, sun-dried them like raisins and popped them back in the body. Then they packed the body cavities with salts and embalming fluid. It was skilled work, but it had no purpose except to preserve dead meat. The pharaohs needed a body in which to enjoy life in the afterworld.

Then came morbid anatomy, which is the art of dissecting bodies to learn how they work. Galen pioneered it in Greece in the 1st century BC, using the bodies of primates.

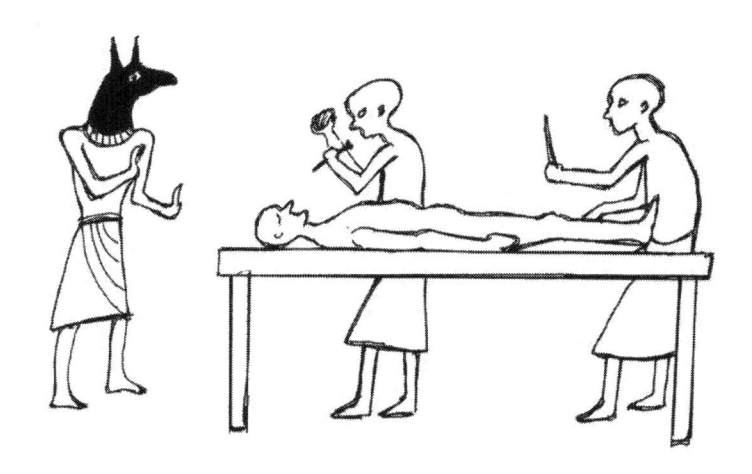

Preserving dead meat

Galen discovered that, contrary to traditional teaching, arteries carried blood and not air. On the downside he popularized the nonsensical theory of the four humours. The theory claimed that good health depended on a balance between blood, phlegm, black bile and yellow bile, whatever they were exactly. The theory stifled medical research for 1,300 years.

Dissections took a forensic turn in Renaissance Italy, which was as murderous a place to live as most South American cities. You never knew who was trying to kill you or how. Imagine, for example, that your great-aunt Donatella dined with the Medici family and later developed excruciating abdominal pain and died. Were the oysters responsible or was it arsenic in the pasta? Her relatives would pay an anatomist to find the answer.

The autopsy often took place in the vault of the church where the funeral was held, which must have made the day a lot longer and more stressful for the mourners. Leonardo da Vinci learned his anatomy this way and claimed to have dissected thirty bodies.

In Britain, surgeons in the 18th century performed dissections to improve their manual dexterity and to earn money. Staging a public anatomy demonstration paid better than setting bones. The body snatchers supplied the surgeons' needs by digging up fresh corpses. Autopsies became legal when the Anatomy Act was passed in 1832, but it was a long time before there were enough professionals to do the work. Until the 1950s a coroner could direct a GP with no training to dissect one of his patients, which was like asking a toddler to perform brain surgery.

Today, the majority of post-mortem examinations are performed by consultant histopathologists working in NHS hospitals. There are 1,500 of them but not all of them relish the work and many let their colleagues get on with it. Either way it is not the major part of their job descriptions.

Most of the examinations are requested by local coroners. A coroner's concern is to establish beyond doubt who the dead person was, when they died, where they died and the cause of their death. (It is not to apportion blame.) If they cannot do this, or if the death was unnatural, they must hold an inquest.

Many a dead body comes to autopsy simply because that person did not see a doctor in his or her final two weeks, which leaves the doctor legally unable to write a death certificate. The lesson is obvious: if you feel a heart attack or stroke coming on, give your GP a call and save everyone a lot of trouble.

The other main category of coroners' cases is sudden, violent and unnatural deaths. If you have the misfortune to die this way, your body goes straight to the mortuary, and you will not escape being dissected. If there is any suspicion of foul play, a forensic (Home Office) pathologist will be called in.

There are barely three dozen of these experts in the country. They undergo years of extra training and have specialized skills and knowledge but, contrary to what you see on TV, they are not all-knowing and all-seeing. To my mind they lead unenviable lives. Everything they do carries the fragrance of death. They live it, breathe it, lecture on it, and write textbooks and thrillers about it. Being independent contractors, they have no employer to care for their mental health and welfare. Dr Richard Shepherd was one of Britain's leading forensic pathologists. In his autobiography *Unnatural Causes,* he discusses the cumulative effects of the 23,000 autopsies that he performed over thirty years. Post-traumatic stress disorder caught up with him and virtually ended his career.

The police are very good at sensing foul play in cases of sudden death, and I only once got out of my depth and had to ask for Home Office help. A middle-aged housewife was found dead in her home in Taunton. The walls, ceiling and furniture of the hall were deluged in blood.

When I entered the mortuary, I saw that we had company. Several police officers with silver braid on their caps stood around. One said, 'We believe it's an accident, doctor, but we'd like to be sure.'

I proceeded cautiously, conscious of the audience. The bleeding was caused by a deep head wound with an underlying skull fracture. At the end of the autopsy, I could not say whether she had fallen and hit her head or had been struck by an assailant. I asked for a police car to take me to the house. The scene was straight out of a *Hammer* horror film. But I could make no sense of it and was none the wiser for the visit.

At this point a senior police officer informed me that the lady's husband was a police sergeant and there was a 'domestic history.' I realised that withholding that information was his idea of not influencing me, while at the same time saving the considerable expense of calling in a forensic specialist.

I was not pleased. 'I can take this no further,' I said. 'You need a Home Office man.'

He arrived the next day. He was a delightful doctor of retirement age whom I knew slightly. He visited the death scene, took a few photographs, and performed a second autopsy. Then he gave me a tutorial.

'Andy, it looks a mess, but it all adds up. She fell down the stairs before hitting her head a terrific blow. That happened on the corner of the telephone table. She fell to the floor, hence the low-level blood splatter on the skirting boards. Then she got up and gyrated, hence the all-round splatter at head height. People with head injuries do that in their confusion. Arterial blood spouts several feet, so there's some on the ceiling too. The vector shows that she staggered into the front room. She collapsed there and bled to death.'

I was impressed, having never given a thought to blood splatter patterns or splatterology, as it is called in the USA. My life had been sheltered, forensically speaking.

Tricky questions arise when relatives are dissatisfied with the care given to their loved one and are looking for someone to blame. The deaths are usually referred to the coroner for a statutory post-mortem.

I was involved in a cluster of such cases when a scandal erupted at the Royal Devon and Exeter Hospital in the 1980s. A tele-cobalt machine which was used to give gamma irradiation to cancer patients was wrongly calibrated, and more than 150 of them received too high a dose. The error came to light when a nurse noted that they suffered skin burns during treatment.

When some of these patients died, the question arose whether excess irradiation had hastened or even caused their deaths. Not surprisingly the Exeter pathologists did not want to get involved in lawsuits against their own colleagues. I was asked, as a disinterested party in another town, to perform the autopsies and report to the Torbay coroner. Over a score of bodies were shuttled between Exeter and Taunton and they involved me in a lot of work. Luckily I had gathered some experience of radiation toxicity during my time in the USA. In nearly all the cases I concluded that the calibration error did not make a significant difference to the outcome.

So much for coroner's cases. Other post-mortems performed in a hospital mortuary are requested by the clinicians. They pose questions that go beyond the simple question 'What did he or she die off?' For example, the physicians may say, 'We knew the diagnosis, why was the treatment not working?' Or the surgeons may say, 'The operation was successful; why did the patient collapse and die?'

The number of clinician requests is dwindling, partly because of the belief that scans and MRIs (magnetic resonance images) make them superfluous. I am not convinced that this is true; when I was in practice, surveys showed that up to a third of clinicians' provisional diagnoses were either inaccurate or incomplete when compared with the post-mortem findings. And they were not the kind of errors that scans and MRIs could detect.

Another reason for the decline in clinicians' autopsies is that hospital managers oppose them on the grounds of cost. They also dismiss as valueless anything that is not subject to a government target. A junior manager once made a financial audit of the pathology service in Taunton. I was clinical director at the time, and he came to me with a puzzled face.

'Dr Adam, why does your department spend so much money on patients who are admitted under the care of other consultants?'

I had to explain what an autopsy was (he had no idea), and that the money was not wasted. He seemed unconvinced until I assured him: 'We only do them on dead people.'

It would be handy if all post-mortem examinations were conclusive, but that is not the case. It is not an exact science. There is no such thing as an absolute cause of death, unless you count extreme cases like decapitation.

A pathologist arrives at a cause of death by a process of elimination. Once his deliberations are complete, he will have a short list; if he's lucky, this is only two or three items long. If there is only one, it is still only the most probable cause, his best guess. Occasionally he will admit that he cannot find a cause and hand the responsibility back to the coroner.

When there are several possibilities, he must judge which is most relevant. Consider the case of a man with a gun shot wound to the head and a failing heart. His heart condition could have killed him at any time. But if the gun wound could have polished off an elephant, the heart condition is incidental. It is something the man died *with* but did not die *of*.

Captain Key's coronary arteries posed this riddle in the Trident aircraft disaster. Soon after arriving in Taunton, I dealt with a case which illustrated it on a far smaller scale. An elderly man was found dead in his car in his garage. A garden hose led from the exhaust pipe to the interior of the car.

The constable who attended the post-mortem scoffed at my involvement. 'It's a no-brainer, Doc. Carbon monoxide poisoning. The old boy lost his wife, and the neighbours say he was depressed. Don't know why you bother.'

'That's the coroner's decision not mine,' I replied stiffly. 'Did he leave a note?'

'No, but they don't always, do they?'

The man's skin had none of the cherry red colour that is typical of carbon monoxide poisoning, nor did his internal organs. But I found a pneumonia that oozed pus.

I tried to establish the circumstances under which the body was found, but the answers conflicted. Nobody could remember turning off the car's ignition, which raised the question of whether it was ever turned on. The man's carboxyhaemoglobin level was minimally raised, which added to the mystery.

The policeman thought that the exercise was academic. I disagreed. Every suicide creates a tempest of emotions for families, colleagues and friends. Sorrow, regret, guilt and recriminations may plague them for decades.

The man had clearly planned his death but who could fathom his state of mind in his final moments? He might have undergone a change of heart. He might never have turned the ignition on. Or he might have turned it on and died from pneumonia before enough gas got into his blood to kill him.

I phoned the coroner, a local solicitor with whom I was on good terms, and told him that the word suicide would not appear in my report. He agreed and returned a verdict of natural causes.

* * *

A pathologist will turn his work to maximum benefit if he can and when I started at Musgrove Park Hospital I wanted to participate in an organ donation scheme. A famous London hospital operated an organ bank which received hearts that came mainly from road accident victims. The valves were dissected out and supplied to cardio-thoracic units throughout Europe and beyond. The protocol for obtaining consent from the next of kin and for handling the hearts was, as you can imagine, governed by strict rules.

I familiarized myself with all the arrangements. But when our first donor, a road accident victim, arrived in the mortuary there was a problem. He had an organ donation card but no known next of kin. The police made inquiries, but nobody came forward. Time was running out and in my enthusiasm I decided to proceed nonetheless. A motorcycle rider was instructed to take the refrigerated box to the railway station. I told him, 'There's no hurry. I've spoken to the staff and they'll take care of it.'

Unfortunately, the rider had a heightened sense of melodrama. He ignored my instruction and persuaded the station master to flag down the next train. A local headline ran, 'Torbay Express held up for mystery heart.' It nearly stopped mine and for days I flinched whenever the phone rang, expecting it to be the General Medical Council or the police. I did not break the rules again.

In those days hospital pathologists dealt with every kind of natural death, including complex conditions like brain tumours, degenerative diseases, congenital diseases and cot deaths. Today they are referred to specialist centres. Without question it was a laudable change which has raised standards and greatly improved the understanding of these conditions.

However, there was one area in which I did some good. Sudden infant death syndrome (or cot death) was far commoner than today. In 1988 nearly 1,600 babies under the age of one year died from it; today the figure is under 300 deaths. There was considerable ignorance and misunderstanding among the public, the media and the police. The stigma of neglect and worse hung over cot deaths. I knew of one case when a father was arrested on the spot and put in a police cell. In the early 2000s several British mothers who had been convicted of murdering their infants had their verdicts quashed.

A young couple who sounded desperate telephoned me. 'We lost our baby two months earlier,' they said. 'The police have questioned us repeatedly and won't say anything. The newspapers say the Criminal Investigation Department (CID) is involved. But there's no talk of an inquest and we have no idea of what's happening.'

The longer the silence continued, the greater the cloud of suspicion. I realised there was a serious disconnection between the authorities and the couple. And legally I was not supposed to discuss the case with either.

I rang the coroner. 'Look Michael,' I said, 'every couple has the right to have their baby's death investigated thoroughly. If there's no blame, can't we tell them the results as soon as possible? And who better to do it than me? But my hands are tied because I can only report to you.'

He saw the point and allowed me to contact those parents – and other bereaved parents in future – as soon as possible. Those meetings were some of my toughest but most rewarding moments in medicine. They usually took place in the home of a couple who were young enough to be my children. I felt a kind of protective fatherly feeling. Their child had died 24 or 48 hours earlier and an empty cot stood in a corner of the room. My task was to tell them firstly that everyone involved – the pathologist, the mortuary technicians, the police and the undertakers – had treated their baby with every care and respect.

I also assured them, if I could, that their baby displayed no injuries and appeared in every way loved and cherished. Most importantly, there was nothing they could have done to prevent the tragedy. That was certainly true at that time; today we know far more about the factors that predispose to cot deaths like sleeping position, overheating and parental smoking.

It was pioneering work in a small way. Today disseminating the information about a cot death is considered of paramount importance. Everyone from the family to the authorities, doctors, midwives, nurses, health visitors and even the media are made aware.

* * *

Regarding the social importance of autopsies, let me tell you what happens in a society in which they are banned for religious or social reasons. That was the situation in Imperial China before the Revolution of 1911-12. For centuries a law called the Custom of Four Thousand Years prevented Chinese doctors from dissecting bodies, even those of murder victims. Ancestor worship demanded reverence for the dead. They could only enter the spirit world if their bodies were intact, give or take a finger or two.

The result was stagnation. There were no dissections, experiments or observations. A Chinese doctor in 1900 knew a lot about the herbal remedies he used, but less anatomy, physiology and medicine than Hippocrates in 450 BC. The arrival of autopsies and other scientific methods from the West changed that.

Now here's an example closer to home. As late as the 1880s, surgeons on both sides of the Atlantic had no idea what caused appendicitis nor how to treat it. They did not even give it the right name. They believed that several different conditions were involved and gave them descriptive labels, none of which was remotely helpful: *perityphlitism, paratyphlitis, peritophlebitis, intestinal affection, colic* and *inflammation of the bowels*.

In a case of acute appendicitis a surgeon would wait for an abscess to point, and if it did he might or might not drain it. Countless patients, many of them young and healthy, died without receiving the right treatment. They included Leon Gambetta who was prime minister of France in 1882. The finest surgeons and physicians in the land stood round his bed arguing while the poor man died in agony from appendicitis. He was only 44.

Around this time the professor of pathology at Massachusetts General Hospital was an energetic and thoughtful doctor called Reginald Fitz. He performed autopsies on 257 patients who died from peritonitis and showed that the process started with what he called 'perforating inflammation' of the appendix. Then he compared those cases with 209 other cases which had been given those strange names and found they were the same condition. He introduced the term *appendicitis* which was entirely new. In a ground-breaking paper written in 1886 he gave his surgical colleagues a master class in treatment. Don't wait for an abscess to form, Fitz said. Act swiftly and remove the cause!

All this reminds me of the world's oldest anatomical theatre. It was built in Padua in Italy in 1594, and over its entrance is a Latin inscription: *Hic locus est ubi mors gaudet succurrere vitae.* It means, 'This is the place where death delights to help the living.'

I cannot close without saying a word about the funeral directors whom I observed at work over many years. I greatly admired them and their staff. With rare exceptions, they were conscientious, polite and knowledgeable in their work and always helpful. One Taunton firm, on hearing about the impending marriage of my daughter Kate in the spring of 1995, generously offered to provide us with one of their vehicles. The poor lass feared she was getting married in a hearse. But on the big day a gleaming black Daimler limousine drew up, adorned with flowers, and driven by a smartly-dressed chauffeur in a peaked cap. It was a lovely gesture.

There were also undertakers of a different kind — single-handed builders who did it on the cheap when the building trade was slack. It was a common practice in West Country villages before big corporations took over the undertaking business. Builders had the necessary muscle, premises and transport. The problem was the paperwork; between jobs they forgot how to do it properly and caused the mortuary staff much extra work. One local builder from Taunton also farmed, and he used his cattle truck to transport bodies – thus bringing straw, mud and country smells into the mortuary. Fortunately he did not last long.

21

Coping (and not Coping)

Over the years people sometimes asked me, 'What's the most unpleasant sort of case you deal with?' For me it was one in which a body's anatomy had been mostly destroyed and the various parts were unrecognizable. I would say to my questioner, 'Please spare a thought for the police and the paramedics and the firemen who are first on the spot. They're not trained for that sort of thing.'

We pathologists become hardened to house fires, explosions, railway suicides, motorway crashes, electrocution, drowning, and hanging as well as putrefaction, liquefaction, and maggots. But if you retain two ounces of humanity there's always something that upsets you, and I think that is a good thing. One should never be indifferent to suffering. I once heard a pathologist boast that, if required to do so, he would have no problem in performing an autopsy on his wife. I do not know which shocked me more: his lack of humanity, or what I imagined was the state of his marriage. I hoped his wife never heard him say it, or she might have made a pre-emptive strike.

Other deaths that upset me were ones that caused undoubted terror to the victims in their final moments. I found myself reliving the events in my mind's eye.

I remember a car on the Somerset Levels carrying five young foreign fruit pickers. It slid into a drainage ditch one night – nobody answered their cries – and they took hours to drown. And a schoolboy on a bicycle who tried to overtake a lorry on the inside and fell under its wheels. He was so small and the lorry so huge that the driver was unaware of what had happened until he was overtaken and stopped. I still remember the face of a toddler who drowned in six inches of water some fifty years ago, while his mother was in the kitchen a few yards away, washing dishes.

How can tragedies like these not leave a mark on a person's soul, even on a pathologist's? For in a mortuary, you deal with real people and real death. You are not in the fictional world of television where the professionals are devoid of feelings and there is neither regret nor remorse.

* * *

People also asked, 'How on earth do you cope?' Again, I would counter with another question. What about the police, the paramedics, the firemen and the nurses? How do they cope? They witness the death throes of the dying and hear their cries. We pathologists have it relatively easy. The victims are past suffering when they reach us.

But the question of coping is valid and yes, there are things that help. The French have an expression *faire bon figure,* which means to put a good face upon something. You get accustomed to the sights and smells. You grow a protective layer and put on a good face.

Everyone in stressful occupations, from bank managers to midwives, develops coping strategies. In the mortuary they are mainly about focus. I demonstrated anatomy to medical students, nursing students, probationary police officers and even 40 Commando Royal Marines from the nearby Norton Manor Camp. And in each case I would say, 'Focus on the problem, ask any questions you like, and we'll get through this together.' Once they got over the shock of seeing a body opened up, they were intrigued and keen to help solve the problem.

Problem? Yes, because to put it bluntly every corpse poses a disposal problem. The relatives, the GP, the undertaker, the coroner and the police all need a cause of death. Only a pathologist can provide it.

Humour helps. There are two kinds of humour to consider: mortuary humour and gallows humour. One is benign and the other is not. Gallows humour makes fun of horrible things in ways that shock and scandalize. They dull our compassion and diminish our humanity. You cannot allow that in a mortuary; it is the start of a slippery slope.

Mortuary humour does not cross that line; it is tempered with respect. The butt of a joke is the context, not the dead person. The humour evolves out of the circumstances. Someone, usually a technician, spots the lighter side of a situation and makes a comment that draws the sting out of it, as in the road tragedy at Ely which I described. It lightens the atmosphere so that people relax and can think more easily. They also absorb information better.

Humour also increases efficiency and productivity, both of which are factors not normally considered in mortuary work. Studies have shown that in workplaces where laughter and banter are permitted, teams are more efficient than those that work in silence.

A nice example of mortuary humour is the last words of Dr William Palmer, a serial murderer in Victoria's reign and one of the greatest villains ever to be tried at the Old Bailey. When he was led onto the scaffold, he eyed the trapdoor and asked, 'Are you sure it's safe?'

Another example (albeit in an operating theatre) occurred after an assassination attempt on President Ronald Reagan. He was seriously wounded and rushed to the nearest hospital. As he was wheeled into the theatre, he removed his oxygen mask and said to the staff, 'I hope you're all Republicans.'

Regarding humour, it is important to remember that every corpse in a mortuary fridge was once somebody's child. Each one was loved and cherished at one time, or so we ought to assume. When I was in practice, I insisted that dead people were not stripped of their identity and that each retained their name and the prefix of Mr, Mrs or Miss. They were not just 'the body in fridge four.' And gallows jokes were out.

Another way to reduce tension in a mortuary is with music. Surgeons play background music when they are operating, so why not pathologists? The mortuary in Taunton stood away from the hospital block and a little music bothered nobody, though I do not recall that we played much. The technicians favoured Radio One when they were clearing up.

I sometimes provided locum cover at our sister hospital in Yeovil, where the mortuary was in the basement. Steve Maurice, the anatomy technician, was a fine baritone who sang in the local operatic company. One day he was practising a few hymns, unaware that a new ventilation duct led close to the operating theatres. The phone rang. Would he please cease singing *Nearer my God to Thee*. The anaesthetists were not amused.

* * *

A good piece of basic advice for anyone in a stressful occupation is not to take their worries home. This is known by a clumsy term, compartmentation, and it requires a conscious effort. I would get home tired and grim.

'Bad day at the office, darling?'

'Uh-huh.'

'Anything to tell me?'

'Nope.' Lesson number one: do not unload your burdens on your wife.

'How about a cup of tea?'

'Yes please. And how was your day?'

Often when I dealt with a child of the same age as one of our own, I would go quietly into my bedroom, close the door and count my blessings.

Do all pathologists cope? No, but nor does every GP or nurse. Most pathologists have a weak spot; mine included a tendency to gag at stomach contents which the technicians found very amusing. For years I could not face eating offal: liver and kidney were definitely off the menu. Funnily enough, I had enjoyed eating them before becoming a pathologist and did so once I retired.

Everybody has a breaking point. If they reach it and if they are sensible, they will quit that job and try something else. Or they may grow an extra layer of callus and carry on at a price.

Let me explain what I mean by a price. Professor Bernard Knight was a legend in forensic medicine. I met him once or twice and greatly admired him. He was a Home Office pathologist for 43 years and performed more than 25,000 autopsies. They included the Frederick West murders and mass exhumations in the Balkans and in Rwanda. He was the first pathologist to use DNA to confirm the identity of a murder victim. He wrote more than thirty thrillers.

More than twenty years ago I heard him being interviewed on BBC radio and I was so intrigued that I wrote and obtained a transcript. He was asked how he coped with his work and answered, 'I get up at 8.00 a.m., do the day's work, wash my hands and go home. Then I see what's on TV.' Clearly Professor Knight knew all about compartmentation.

But his view of human nature was rock bottom. I quote the interview verbatim: 'Humanity stinks! The human race is pretty rotten and the more I see of it the more rotten it becomes. We are a malignancy on the face of the earth. Look at the things we have done to the environment and the animal kingdom.'

He went on, 'I'm a devout atheist. Religion is a form of mental aberration ... When you're dead you rot and that's all there is.' He admitted to having nightmares with which he could not cope. Not surprisingly, perhaps.

If, as I suspect, Professor's Knight's views of humanity and religion were shaped in part by his work, that is a high price to pay.

22

Murder at Sea

'Dr Adam, is there such a thing as a perfect murder?' The questioner was a middle-aged lady with a blue rinse and a glint in her eye. We were at a dinner party many years ago and her husband, who was not present, was conducting an affair with a woman half his age.

I chose my words with care. 'I doubt it. A perfect murder is simply one that's not yet been solved. There's an amazing new invention called DNA analysis. The police recently solved a murder case long after ...'

'Yes, yes, I know about that!' she snapped. 'But how would you go about committing a perfect murder?'

A court room response was the best way to get her to drop the subject. 'I'm sorry. That's outside my area of expertise.'

Thanks to the distortions inherent in TV crime series and crime thrillers, the myth persists that pathologists spend all their time dissecting murder victims and helping the police find the killer. The truth is that most hospital pathologists have little experience of murder and no more interest in it than the average curate.

I was called upon to perform autopsies on murder victims a few times. On each occasion a jealous husband killed his wife and turned the shotgun on himself. No criminal charges could possibly result and (as in the case of the police sergeant's wife) the police wanted to save the cost of a forensic expert.

I found those cases extremely depressing. Children, families and friends were devastated, and communities stricken. When you consider the consequences of a single murder, it is astonishing that murder and mayhem have become the staple diet of our entertainment industry. Why do we allow ourselves to be amused and diverted by something so dark and negative? Perhaps deep down we all fear the possibility of being murdered. Or perhaps we dream the unthinkable – that we may commit one.

It was not always so. For nearly 2,000 years, from Aristotle to Shakespeare, murder was depicted as tragedy. The Greek plays were designed to produce compassion for the victim, and pity and charity towards a murderer if he showed remorse. The tragedies brought a healing catharsis to the audience, together with a fear of the gods and a resolve to shun violence. You don't see much of that on television today.

In my mind murder is always 'murder most foul.' However, I was persuaded to take an interest in one killer and to study him in depth. To explain how that came about I must go back to 2010, when Jacqui caught pneumonia. To speed her recovery, we booked a cruise in the Caribbean. It was our first cruise and rather to my surprise it proved fun. We particularly enjoyed the guest speakers. They give illustrated talks on the days when a ship is at sea.

Two experts from the Tate Modern Gallery spoke on 18th century family portraits, a topic to which I had never given a thought. They brought it to life with passion and humour. Another speaker spoke on shipwrecks, which have a certain fascination when you are miles from land. Another was a retired CID sergeant.

Jacqui read my thoughts. 'Why not try it darling? You've time on your hands. You know about medicine and history and you like telling stories. Then you can take me on holidays which we can't afford!' She beamed.

The expert on shipwrecks instructed me how to navigate the vetting and audition process of the company which owns the Cunard Line and P&O Cruises. The theme of my talks was *Matters of Life and Death*. That allowed me to offer a wide variety of subjects including serial killers, TV crime drama, near-death experiences, the chronic grief syndrome, English eccentrics, medical humour and the Boxer Rebellion of 1900 in which my grandfather nearly perished.

* * *

I passed the tests, and in consequence Jacqui and I enjoyed many years of wonderful voyages on liners and cruise ships all over the world. We travelled tens of thousands of sea miles and I often revisit the places in my mind: the fire mountains of Iceland, the jungles of South America, the glittering palaces of St. Petersburg, tiny fishing villages on the Adriatic, and the grand approach to the Panama Canal.

Cruising enthusiasts are often mocked, but not all do it simply to float, bloat and booze. We met some outstandingly interesting people, particularly other guest speakers on the North Atlantic crossings: theatrical directors, academics and authors. American cosmonauts are particularly good company. They are the nearest thing to royalty that the Americans have.

I soon discovered that it was one thing to be accepted as a guest speaker; it was another to become an expert. Doctors are trained to teach: to impart information without the frills and with only a modicum of humour. Guest speakers have to entertain their audience, to develop a rapport and win smiles and chuckles. The jackpot is what the Spanish call *una carcajada*, a belly laugh.

I worked hard and my talks were well received and often attracted a full house. I sometimes wondered if that was because of my magnetic charm, but I concluded that most people have a fascination with death, even if they rarely admit to it. Habitual cruisers tend to be elderly, and many are widowed, so my talks on near-death experiences and chronic grief found a natural audience. The average age on one Mediterranean cruise was 69 and the gentleman with whom I shared shouted exchanges over the dinner table was 91.

A guest speaker also needs to be able to take disappointment. You compete with every conceivable activity on board a cruise ship, from aromatherapy to zumba. And everyone wants to get a suntan. How do you persuade them to leave a swimming pool in gorgeous weather for a darkened theatre? It is like prizing barnacles off a rock. But when the storm clouds gather and the Atlantic gales blow, you may have a captive audience of hundreds.

When storm clouds gather

Jacqui enjoyed my performances for a particular reason. She would sit in the audience like a covert spy, listening to the conversations around her. As my talk concluded, she'd turn to them and remark, 'That's my husband actually. Would you like to meet him?' And they would become quite flustered, and often want to come along and be introduced.

Our maiden voyage was aboard Queen Mary II from Southampton to New York. On the first day out, she battled against winds of 70 knots and waves seven metres high. At breakfast the captain announced over the loudspeaker: 'Ladies and gentlemen, the Queen Mary was built for North Atlantic gales; she cuts through them like butter. There's no cause for alarm. Please enjoy your day.'

The officers may have enjoyed the storm up on the bridge, but below the waterline things were different. Queen Mary II has an art deco auditorium the size of a London theatre. Usually it feels solid, but that day it heaved like a contralto's bosom. The stabilisers could not cope, and the curtains shot from one side of the stage to the other. The groans coming from the hull sounded like souls in torment.

On the stage I clutched the lectern to prevent myself toppling off. Why on earth had they not cancelled my talk? Passengers tottered in. Their expressions said, 'To hell with the weather, we want our money's worth.' They fumbled along the rails to their seats.

I was anxious for a good reason. Guest speakers' talks are broadcast live on television screens in cabins, lounges and cocktail bars. If my breakfast chose to come up, the moment would be caught throughout the entire ship.

The minute hand reached the twelve. I tapped the microphone, smiled as brightly as I could and launched into my talk. The topic was as nauseous as the weather, but the show must go on.

The subject was Dr Harold Shipman, the most prolific serial killer in Britain in modern times. In 2000 he was convicted at Preston Crown Court of murdering fifteen patients by injecting them with morphine. A judicial enquiry subsequently found he killed at least 215 patients, with another 45 probable cases. Thus, during the course of thirty years he committed at least 215 'perfect murders.' Then he grew overconfident and made a mistake. His score dropped to zero.

I shall not weary you with Shipman's *modus operandi* or how he covered his tracks for so long. It is the man who intrigues me. As Sherlock Holmes remarks in *The Adventure of the Speckled Band,* 'When a doctor goes wrong, he is the first of criminals. He has the nerve and he has the knowledge.' Shipman had both in abundance.

When I decided to research his career, it was not simply because of the enormity of his crimes, but because of their effect upon my profession. He seriously damaged the basis of trust between patients and their GPs; he changed the way the latter were regarded, and he contributed to a culture of blame. He deterred – and still deters – many doctors from using opiate drugs in situations where they are proper and safe to use.

During his first job in general practice, Shipman became addicted to pethidine and took to forging prescriptions until he was discovered. He had already started killing patients, so disbarring him for drug offences would have saved many lives. Instead, he was fined £600 by a magistrates' court. The General Medical Council failed to discipline him, and he found his way back into general practice.

In the town of Hyde, outside Manchester, Shipman became to all appearances a model physician, the best GP in town. He had an admirable bedside manner, being obliging, friendly and unhurried. He was good with children, expectant mothers and elderly ladies. He flirted mildly with the latter and encouraged them to call him by his first name. Not surprisingly he had a long waiting list.

The very people who appreciated him most were literally dying to meet him. They were mainly widows and spinsters living on their own. They had arthritis, heart symptoms and other ailments but they were coping. They lived in council flats and back-to-backs and kept cats and budgies. They shopped and went to church and bingo. They had children and grandchildren who loved them.

We will never know why he selected some patients and not others. He had no reason to hate elderly ladies. They were not bed-ridden or from suffering from a terminal illness. Their sole fault was that they trusted him and were not in a position to question him. Some he may have found irksome, but others gave him no trouble and regarded him as their friend. Yet he killed them all the same.

Shipman was addicted to murder, just as a person becomes addicted to alcohol or gambling. The more you have, the more you want. At first he indulged in one or two murders which were followed by a cooling off interval. The intervals got progressively shorter until things spiralled out of control. By 1998 he was dispatching two or three victims a week. Yet even after he was arrested and charged, patients could not accept that their much-loved doctor was a killer.

He always protested his innocence and refused to cooperate with the court that convicted him. In 2004 he hanged himself in Wakefield prison, taking his secrets to the grave.

What drove him to such murderous exploits? Most serial killers lead lives that are dysfunctional and chaotic. Shipman had a stable marriage with four children, and he functioned well in a demanding profession. Serial killers are often violent, but he was not. The deaths he caused were gentle and pain-free. There was no significant profit motive and no evidence that he derived any sexual gratification. A psychologist found no evidence of schizophrenia or other mental disorder.

For clues we must go back to his youth. Shipman was born in 1946 in Nottingham where his father was a lorry driver and his mother Vera worked in a laundry. He was the middle child of three and Vera idolized him. She seems to have given him the idea that he was special and could achieve anything.

When she was 43, she was diagnosed with lung cancer. It advanced rapidly and he helped to nurse her during her last months. He watched the GP inject her with morphine to relieve her pain and bring her sleep. He may have administered some injections himself.

After her death, he vowed to become a doctor and worked hard to achieve his ambition. But did he become a doctor to help people who suffered like Vera? Or did he do it to exercise control over them, to be the arbiter of their lives and deaths? John Pollard, the South Manchester coroner who knew Shipman, held the second opinion. He wrote, 'The only valid possible explanation is that he simply enjoyed viewing the process of dying and enjoyed the feeling of control over life and death.'

Similarly Dr Richard Badcock, the only psychiatrist who interviewed Shipman, believed that he 'suffered from a spiritual disorder that transcended the conventional diagnoses of medicine, psychiatry and religion.' The factors surrounding his mother's death were important, but Badcock said that it boiled down to one thing. 'It is about evil,' he said.

The idea of evil is not always accepted in a world of moral relativism, but I believe that Pollard and Badcock were right, and that Harold Shipman was an outrageously evil man. He had no moral compass and no room for guilt, conscience or remorse. He was on a level with Joseph Mengele and the other evil Nazi physicians.

Here is an irony with which to finish. If Shipman could speak from the grave, he might claim that he made a positive contribution to medicine. He showed up failings in many areas including death certification, the monitoring of dangerous drugs, the incompetence of the General Medical Council, flaws in the coroner's system and the need for the regular appraisal and revalidation of doctors.

He might also claim that he did a favour to the community in which he worked. He brought relief to the elderly and infirm, because in his view they had ceased to have social value. They were a burden and there was no reason to keep them alive.

That chilling argument is heard today in the euthanasia debate and needs to be rejected firmly and constantly.

Afterword

The years at Musgrove Park Hospital sped by. In the summer of 1993, I had a close shave with death. At the end of a long day I collapsed, and I woke next morning with a throat like red-hot barbed wire. I could not swallow or speak. Our GP was urgently summoned and found me too ill to wait for an ambulance. Jacqui rushed me by car to Musgrove Park, where I passed out.

I came to my senses in strange surroundings. John Swift, the mortuary technician, was bending over me. It took a little time to work out that I was not on a mortuary slab but in ITU, in a bed usually reserved for brain-dead patients. I was hitched to tubes, monitors, drips and oxygen. John was my first visitor. He was running a professional eye over my frame.

After a week of intensive treatment in hospital, I was much recovered and discharged with a diagnosis of acute pharyngo-tracheitis. The laboratory never identified the cause, which was probably a streptococcal infection that I caught off a corpse. Pathologists are prey to whatever is lying around, not just tuberculosis.

After that my thoughts turned from pathology to lighter things. It was a natural progression. No man on his death bed ever wished he had spent more time at his office, nor did any woman wish for more housework. Similarly, no pathologist ever lamented not having done more autopsies.

Soon after my sixtieth birthday in 1999, I took early retirement. Like Shakespeare's Prospero I broke my staff and drowned my book. Medicine moves too fast to keep up while working part-time. And besides, new adventures beckoned.

Over the next twenty years I served as an elder in a lively Pentecostal church and as a street pastor. I served as a police chaplain with the Somerset and Avon Constabulary. I also helped to establish a charity that places volunteer chaplains in workplaces, care homes and law courts, and I was its first chairman. I continued to write, produced a couple of books, and enjoyed the challenge of bible teaching, the company of my exceptional family, and the arrival of six beloved grandchildren.

Then there were the cruise ships, until Covid put a stop to them. When the pandemic was over, I did not want to go back. After twenty cruises I was in danger of falling asleep during my own talks. Since then my life has become more reflective, and I am happiest working on a book, preparing some bible teaching or pottering around the garden.

I sometimes think about my 'legacy'. I held no public office, participated in no great historical events and won no medals. I made no medical discoveries; all the scientific papers I wrote are out of date and my non-medical books will be forgotten in time. I leave behind a pharmacist's antique chest, a Victorian brass microscope, Betty in her box in the attic and an old pair of white mortuary boots which I use for gardening.

But Jacqui and I have a sound legacy. It lies in our children and our grandchildren. We have sowed into them all, and our reward is watching these amazing individuals become firmly rooted in their own Christian faith, living lives full of love and purpose.

I am in my 85th year and my contemporaries are dropping like flies. At times it seems that I shall be the last one left standing. That's another reason for writing this book. Perhaps the ones who are still above ground will read and take note of these final pages.

As a society we are losing our sense of reality about death. We are not just detached; we are becoming indifferent. An American preacher called James Coffman had plenty of time to consider the matter. He reached the age of one hundred before dying in 2006.

Coffman wrote, 'Death is an ugly problem for man, but how does he face up to it? He will not even speak of it. Even when the last agony is upon him, his physician will hardly tell him the truth; his wife assures him that he is better; and even his minister speaks of what he will do when he gets well. What a tragic blindness it is that forces the great, the intelligent, the prominent and powerful on earth to go on living as if death had no claim upon them.'

Medical science makes everything seem possible and people are determined to enjoy life indefinitely. We have sanitised the language of death in the hope of immortality. Even the words death and dying are taboo. When a person dies, they 'pass on,' 'pass over' or 'pass away.' In the same way they kick the bucket, fall off the perch, join the great majority or take some other euphemistic way out of life.

Death itself is hidden away. In my grandparents' day most people died at home with their family around them. The women washed and dressed the corpse and laid it in an open coffin. Voices were hushed, curtains were drawn, and the house was filled with flowers. Everybody came to pay their respects, including the children.

Funerals were events that you did not miss. A whole village or street accompanied the cortège on foot to the church. Cremations were rare. A period of mourning was observed to show respect for the dead person and to give people the opportunity to contemplate their mortality.

Some of that still happens in remote parts of the British Isles, but the statistics are reversed. Today four out of five people die in hospitals, nursing homes and hospices. The bodies are whisked away and dealt with professionally. They may never be seen again by the family members.

Most bodies are cremated, and the church has been replaced by the crematorium chapel, where the atmosphere is informal to the point of nonchalance. I have attended services when the coffin arrived to Rod Stewart singing *Embraceable You* and left to *Wish Me Luck as You Wave Me Goodbye*. The most popular choice in Britain for many years has been Frank Sinatra doing things his way.

And a period of mourning? Oh no, that's old fashioned and unnecessary. You may get invited to tea and sandwiches back at the house, or even down at the pub. And black is out. The focus has become all about the celebration of life.

Please do not misunderstand me. As a doctor, I want everyone to enjoy the best quality of life for as long as they can. But I am concerned at the widespread culture of denial. It means that we minimize or reject anything that disturbs our peace of mind, including irreversible changes in our bodies. We avoid taking steps that admit that we will die, like seeking forgiveness and reconciliation and taking a proper and timely leave of loved ones. And we avoid practical decisions, like making a will or an advance directive or creating a power of attorney.

Let me quote James Coffman again. He wrote: 'The greatest falsehood of the age is the allegation that Christianity is a psychological escape-hatch for defeated and frustrated souls.'

I have dealt with thousands of dead people in my lifetime, but the only comfort I can give is what I have learned through my faith. I declare that that there is no more normal, wholesome and natural way for a person to live than following Jesus. It is how God designed us to live and to die and I have tried the other ways.

Printed in Great Britain
by Amazon